The church of the Lord Jesus is in desperate need for men of God; men who know God, love God and serve God with lives surrendered to his lordship. *Pastoring Men* helps us understand why we must and how we can effectively disciple men in our churches who will become radically devoted followers of our great Savior and King. Biblical and practical, this is a much needed resource for those who long to effectively pastor and raise up an army of godly men.

DANIEL L. AKIN
President, Southeastern Baptist Theological Seminary

Pastoring Men is a realistic, encouraging, and insightful examination of how to develop—and sustain—a first-rate, field-tested method to disciple men. Put this book at the top of your reading list.

JAMES S. BOWMAN
Professor, Florida State University (and chair of Patrick's dissertation committee)
Editor, Public Integrity

I know of no one in America who knows more about men—what they think, want, feel, and believe—than Pat Morley. Not only that, I know of no one who cares more for men and has more passion for discipling them than Pat Morley. If you care about the "men problem" in our culture and the church, this is your book. It is profoundly biblical and incredibly practical. It could change the face of the church and, through the church, the nation.

STEVE BROWN
Professor, Reformed Theological Seminary, Orlando
Teacher on the nationally syndicated radio program Key Life

Pastoring Men directly confronts a critical need in our churches today: developing godly men! The need is great, but so is the opportunity. Our churches must disciple all the men and equip them to succeed at home and in the culture. Pat Morley asks and answers the significant questions that enable pastors to effectively minister to all of their men.

KIRBYJON H. CALDWELL
Windsor Village Methodist Church, Houston

"This is a battle worth fighting." What true words! It is a battle that takes diligent, persistent effort along with even more diligence in prayer and trust in the Lord. It is also a battle worth fighting, especially by pastors. We need more men who are faithful followers of Christ in their homes, churches, jobs, and communities and who can lead and disciple other men, as well as women and children. The Lord has given Pat many insights into the effective discipleship of men. Come join the battle to disciple ongoing generations of godly men.

ROBERT C. (RIC) CANNADA JR.
Former Chancellor and CEO, Reformed Theological Seminary

Patrick Morley's long-standing concern to see the light of Christ in the life of men has always been inspiring. Now this exceedingly practical book helping pastors implement discipleship programs specifically directed toward men will do much to shape the future of home, church, and the next generation. Morley writes in terms that reach men—and change them.

BRYAN CHAPELL
Senior Pastor, Grace Presbyterian Church
Peoria, Illinois

This is more than a book. It is a prophetic word that comes at a pivotal time in our contemporary history. *Pastoring Men* salutes the priority that God designed to be the leading edge of good, new beginnings of reformation and harbingers of hope. It's a clarion call that not only beckons us back to His mandate, but gives us practical ways to follow. This book can renew our churches. It restores the priority of calling men to lead, to be the first to serve, and to be the examples that will direct us back to God's best.

WAYNE CORDEIRO
New Hope Christian Fellowship Foursquare Church, Honolulu

Pastoring Men is written by a man who understands men—their needs, desires, and aspirations. Pat Morley offers a useful plan for any pastor who wants to focus on building a ministry of discipleship for every man in his church. Engaging, inspiring, and practical, *Pastoring Men* has vast potential in the process of discipling men in the local church.

ROD CULBERTSON JR.
Associate professor of practical theology, dean of student development
Reformed Theological Seminary, Charlotte

The information contained in this book is fundamental, biblical, and critical for this day and age. *Pastoring Men* articulates the needs of men both within the church and in representing the church in a secularized society. The church has, in many ways, failed at pastoring men. This book equips leaders to understand the challenge and have a clear vision for the call.

MAURY DAVIS
Senior Pastor, Cornerstone Church of the Assemblies of God
Madison, Tennessee

Every pastor knows that if you reach the man for Christ, you will also more than likely reach the entire family. Consequently, discipling the men in your church is strategic to fulfilling Christ's Great Commission. Patrick Morley's strategy is to disciple men who can impact every arena of life and ministry. This book combines the best of *Man In the Mirror* and *No Man Left Behind* to provide every pastor with the inspiration, strategy, and practical tools to disciple every man in the church. This excellent tool can create a continual flow of called, equipped, and committed lay leaders. It is a resource I and my leadership team will refer to time and time again.

MARK FULLER
Pastor, Grove City Church of the Nazarene

As a pastor to pastors, I believe you need to read this book. You'll discover how important you are in developing a vibrant men's ministry in your church. It won't happen as it should without your direct leadership. You'll discover that the results will permeate every aspect of your ministry.

GENE A. GETZ
Pastor Emeritus, Chase Oaks Church
President, Center for Church Renewal, Plano, Texas

Pat Morley knows men. He's been in the foxholes discipling hundreds for more than twenty years—weeping , teaching, counseling, and challenging them to be all that God wants them to be as husbands, fathers, employees/employers, and effective laymen in the church. As his pastor, I've watched him closely for all these years. He's the real deal. This book is a guide from Scripture to shoe leather to help all of us who are serious about change in our own lives as well as desperate to disciple others.

CHUCK GREEN
Pastor Emeritus, Orangewood Presbyterian Church

I don't think I have encountered a better apologetic for calling men to discipleship than Pat's new book. It gets inside the heart of both pastor and layman and introduces them to each other. Often much is lost in translation between pastor and the average guy; Pat becomes the mediator and translator. Real understanding is the result.

BILL HULL
Author, Jesus Christ, Disciplemaker, The Disciple-Making Church, The Disciple-Making Pastor

Men are indeed the untapped reservoir of useful energy for the kingdom of God. Patrick Morley has been used by the Lord to help men become a vital part of His work in the church and kingdom. No one has more passion for men's ministry than this author. Read *Pastoring Men* and learn from one who knows how!

JOHNNY M. HUNT
Pastor, First Baptist Woodstock
President of Southern Baptist Convention

Pastor, this book will help you to better understand the men in your congregation . . . and to better understand yourself. It will sharpen your church's ministry to men . . . and it will sharpen you. Men are practical. And Patrick Morley is totally practical, but not predictable. Thank you, Patrick, for this invaluable tool!

JOEL C. HUNTER
Senior Pastor of Northland Church

If it were possible, I would give this book to every pastor in America. It's that good and right on target! It powerfully states what every pastor urgently needs to hear, namely, *your men desperately need you to disciple them.* Few men can explain why or how to do this better than Patrick Morley. Let him help you win with your men.

ROBERT LEWIS
Pastor-at-large, Fellowship Bible Church
Founder of Men's Fraternity

Statistics show the decline of participation of men in church. Pat Morley has confronted this situation with candor and compassion. He offers positive perspectives on how the church can reclaim men both in participation and leadership. His approach is extremely practical and very applicable for the local church. Those of us serving in the professional ministry genuinely appreciate this helpful and insightful book.

JOHN ED MATHISON
Author, speaker; johnedmathison.org

Leadership is influence. *Pastoring Men* is an insightful and practical tool to increase your influence with your men. This book will help you create, capture, and sustain the momentum you need to more effectively disciple all the men in your church. Read this book! You won't be disappointed!

JOHN C. MAXWELL
Author, speaker, and founder of ISS and EQUIP
Duluth, Georgia

Pat once again shows us that there is no task more important or urgent than discipling men. *Pastoring Men* shares with us the need, the burden, and the practical steps to "leave no man behind." I urge every pastor to read and apply this book to your life and ministry.

DWAYNE MERCER
Pastor, CrossLife Church, Oviedo, Florida

Patrick Morley has done it again. Just like *Man in the Mirror*, he has written a must read for men and pastors alike. Read it with your eyes, plant it in your heart, and you will be more of God's man than you ever dreamed you could be.

JAMES MERRITT
Lead pastor, Cross Pointe Church, Duluth, Georgia

Patrick Morley knows men. He knows their hopes, their hurts, and their dreams. Now The-Man-in-the-Mirror man provides pastors and other church leaders a tool that may become indispensable in our hurting churches that love hurting men. I commend *Pastoring Men* to you with enthusiasm. I just wish the book had been available when I was a pastor.

THOM S. RAINER
President and CEO, LifeWay Christian Resources, Nashville

The Bible repeatedly uses the phrase "act like men." So clearly there is something about Christian manhood and biblical masculinity that is desired when the gospel takes hold of a man's heart. Patrick Morley has again addressed this issue biblically and profoundly in a way that not only clarifies but also assists pastors and leaders in knowing how to shepherd and disciple men for Christ.

HARRY L. REEDER, III
Senior Pastor, Briarwood Presbyterian Church

Patrick is addressing one of the most critical issues for the church of the twenty-first century. Children will follow in the faith, values, and lifestyles of their fathers. We must engage men in the heroic places of their hearts to lead the next generation as role models of faith and integrity.

MIKE SLAUGHTER
Pastor, Ginghamsburg Church

Drawing from his vast experience, Pat has taken the mystery out of how to connect with, shepherd, and motivate men to be disciples of Jesus Christ. An incredibly insightful and practical work, *Pastoring Men* should be on every pastor's shelf as both blueprint for beginning a compelling men's ministry and as fresh wind to invigorate a stale one. This is a very important book for the kingdom.

JAY SIMMONS
Senior Pastor, Grace + Peace, Austin

As a pastor for fifty-plus years, I had a great desire to help men become the spiritual leaders God intends them to be. The work of Patrick Morley was very helpful to me. This newest book will be invaluable to pastors in that responsibility today. His chapters "What Do Men Want?" and "What Do Men Need?" are worth the price of the book.

JERRY VINES
President, Jerry Vines Ministries
Pastor Emeritus, First Baptist Church, Jacksonville, Florida
Past President, Southern Baptist Convention

Let's be honest: The worst kept secret in our churches is how poorly we're *really* doing at activating and equipping men for the most thrilling, fulfilling, and demanding purpose on the planet: following Jesus. With his new book, *Pastoring Men,* Patrick Morley squarely targets leaders and pastors with that challenge. Jammed with years of insight, "reality-check" statistics, and practical tips on the essential factors for discipling men, *Pastoring Men* gives us enough fire and resources to get it done.

DAVE WORKMAN
Vineyard, Cincinnati, author of The Outward-Focused Life

PASTORING
MEN

WHAT WORKS, WHAT DOESN'T, AND WHY MEN'S
DISCIPLESHIP MATTERS NOW MORE THAN EVER

PATRICK MORLEY

MOODY PUBLISHERS

CHICAGO

All Scripture quotations, unless otherwise indicated, are taken from the *Holy Bible, New International Version*®, NIV®. Copyright © 1973, 1978, 1984, 2011 by Biblica, Inc.™ Used by permission of Zondervan. All rights reserved worldwide. www.zondervan.com. The "NIV" and "New International Version" are trademarks registered in the United States Patent and Trademark Office by Biblica, Inc.™

Scripture quotations marked NASB are taken from the *New American Standard Bible,*® Copyright © 1960, 1962, 1963, 1968, 1971, 1972, 1973, 1975, 1977, 1995 by The Lockman Foundation. Used by permission. (www.Lockman.org)

Scripture quotations marked KJV are taken from the King James Version.

Scripture quotations marked NLT are taken from the *Holy Bible, New Living Translation*, copyright © 1996, 2004. Used by permission of Tyndale House Publishers, Inc., Wheaton Illinois 60189, U.S.A. All rights reserved.

Edited by Jim Vincent
Cover and Interior Design: Smartt Guys design
Cover Image: © David Madison / Getty Images (200026641-001)

Library of Congress Cataloging-in-Publication Data
Morley, Patrick M.
Pastoring men : what works, what doesn't, and why men's discipleship matters now more than ever / Patrick Morley.
    p. cm.
Includes bibliographical references.
ISBN 978-0-8024-1444-1
1. Church work with men. I. Title.
BV4440.M68 2008
259.081--dc22
                    2008035062

We hope you enjoy this book from Moody Publishers. Our goal is to provide high-quality, thought-provoking books and products that connect truth to your real needs and challenges. For more information on other books and products written and produced from a biblical perspective, go to www.moodypublishers.com or write to:

Moody Publishers
820 N. LaSalle Boulevard
Chicago, IL 60610

1 3 5 7 9 10 8 6 4 2

Printed in the United States of America

In memory of ROBERT S. MORLEY
1923–2003

Husband of Alleen
Father of Pat, Robert, Pete, and Bill
A good man, humble, with integrity, and a hard worker

CONTENTS

PROLOGUE

AN OPEN LETTER TO LAYMEN FROM A PASTOR

The following letter is one I'm sure you'd love to send as a pastor—but, of course, you'd never send it. I'm writing it because I want you to know that I understand what you're going through with men.

Though it's fictitious, the letter is based on conversations I have had with hundreds of pastors during the past twenty years. I believe it represents their desire—and yours—to help men become disciples, as well as the frustration in pursuing that goal. It also reflects my passion that this book will equip you with the concepts and strategies you need to more effectively disciple every man in your church.

Dear Laymen,

I would like to get some things off my chest. Since I could never say these things to my own men (and survive), I will say them to you. I offer these thoughts humbly.

Frankly, I get nervous when some of my men get all excited and start talking men's movement lingo like *father wound, masculinity,* etc.

What often happens is that the least-respected men in the church— the ones who talk about Jesus all the time but struggle to keep a job— "take over" the men's ministry. No one would follow them on a bet—I know I wouldn't want to be in a small group they led.

So, honestly, it's just easier for me to let them do what they want. I want to help them, but in my heart I don't really think they have what it takes, and they will eventually peter out and I'll be back to zero—or worse. Don't get me wrong. I love them. And I have faith that God has good plans for them. But, at least at this point, they need to be the minis-terees, not the ministers.

WHAT I CAN GET BEHIND

I'll tell you what I can get behind. I can get behind a disciple-making plan that men I respect are personally involved with.

Let me tell you a secret. If you really want to get me involved, here's what you would do. You would find between six and twelve of the most respected men in the church—normal guys. Invite them to a meeting to explore and pray about reaching more men for Christ. Give me a heads-up *before* this exploratory meeting, so I'm not feeling blindsided. Don't try to take it too fast. Pray a lot. Don't be afraid to ask men for a big commitment.

Once you have some men willing to make a go of it, then come see me. Please. When you do come see me, don't act like you're the first ones who ever thought of reaching the men in our church. I've beaten my head against that wall for years trying to get men more involved.

HOW TO WIN ME OVER

Give me space—and time—to process how it would work. Don't try to "close" me right away. Everyone thinks if they just lean on me hard enough then their program can go. Show me some stats, build the case. Why should I add to, change, or tweak my existing focus?

Ask me how ministry to men can help me. Find out what I think are the problems our men face as husbands, fathers, workers, churchmen, and men in general. I pick up quite a lot, you know, in the course of a day.

And come see me before you have the whole concept designed—I will need to make sure the plans mesh with our vision and other church ministries. Besides, I probably can make a unique contribution as the pastor.

We can meet and discuss why we need to reach men, how men in our church are doing, what kind of men we want to produce, what will constitute success for us, and how we will measure progress.

Make it easy for me to support a ministry to our men. Talk about getting men into small groups to study the Bible. Talk about helping men understand the gospel. Talk about how we can build men up as godly men for the home, church, workplace, and community. Talk about integrating men into the existing ministries of the church. And not just some of our men, but all of them!

Don't talk about adding a bunch of new programming like retreats, seminars, etc. First things first. Let's see how you can help make the ministries we're already committed to work.

JUST SO YOU KNOW WHAT I'M UP AGAINST

Like you, I want to serve God and have a successful ministry. I got into this field because I sensed a calling from God to make a difference for the gospel of Jesus.

The other day someone asked, "Why don't you care about the men in our church?" Why would they think that? It hurts when people question my motives.

I work hard to be an effective leader. The demands are unbelievably diverse—and they excite me. I love the variety of public communication, private counseling, leading a staff, inspiring volunteers, administrating an organization, marriages, baptisms, funerals, committee meetings, and more.

Here's what I see happening when it comes to men's ministries: A man brings me an idea, but often acts like I had nothing else to do but drop everything and embrace his idea . . . an idea he did not do a very good job researching, explaining, or finding others to support. He has no plan. In fact, what he really wants is to dump the whole idea in my lap and be done with it. He thinks I'm the professional so it's my job. Are you surprised that a pastor would speak so bluntly? Don't be. We're human too, and we all feel this way sometimes.

You have no idea how many people let me down. Hey, I'm not feeling sorry for myself, and I'm certainly not angry. Indeed, I thank God for those people who, when they tell me they will get something done, I can bank on it. But often I have not found people to be very dependable. It's as though their word to the church is the first thing that gets cut. Even that wouldn't bother me so much if they would just tell me. As it is, most of the nonperformers don't tell me until the day they were supposed to be finished.

NEVERTHELESS, I WANT TO BUILD
A GROWING CHURCH

So please keep me in your prayers. Think the best of my motives. Help me see that you are really serious about reaching our men. Show me that you don't merely want to start something, and then dump it in my lap.

And by the way, you will have more clout with me if I see that you have a track record of actually ministering to men yourself.

So I'm excited about what we could do together that we could never do alone. I am eager to partner with you to grow Christ's church. When can we get together?

Warmly in Christ,
Your Pastor

1

IS PASTORING MEN
WORTH THE EFFORT?

Much has been made about the "men problem." You can hear about it from Oprah. You can read about it in *Time*. You can watch the destruction it creates with Dr. Phil.

Schoolteachers can barely educate on the heels of it. Social services are overwhelmed because of it. Employers are stumped by it. Law enforcement feels the brunt of it. Many jails and prisons are full because of it. Politicians don't know what to do with it. Candidates avoid it.

Authors and academics have assembled alarming statistics to prove it. Healthcare professionals publish convincing reports to document the human cost of it. Cable shows rant at it. Talk radio personalities have all the answers for it. Movies glamorize it. Television commercials mock it.

The "men problem." Divorce courts are at capacity because of it. Families are ripped apart by it. Wives soak their pillows with tears as a result of it. Children grow up in poverty as a consequence of it. Teenagers experiment with drugs and sex to cope with it.

A lot of money gets spent to treat the symptoms of it. We open teenage pregnancy centers, start divorce recovery groups, establish substance abuse centers, increase budgets for social services, build homes for battered women, authorize more jail space, put extra beds in our homeless shelters, increase the number of law enforcement officers, and fit our schools with metal detectors to deal with it.

Everyone is concerned about it. Many address the consequences of it. Yet very few people are doing anything that will change the root of it. The "men problem" is among the most pervasive social, economic, political, and spiritual problems of all time.

As I wrote in my book *Man Alive,* the statistics are jarring:

- 80 percent of men are so emotionally impaired that not only are they unable to *express* their feelings, but they are even unable to *identify* their feelings.[1]
- 60 percent of men are in financial trouble, paying only the monthly minimums on their credit card balances.[2]
- 50 percent of men who attend church actively seek out pornography.[3]
- 40 percent of men get divorced, affecting one million children each year.[4]

The conclusion is inescapable: *Men have become one of our largest neglected people groups.* As a result, they are prone to get caught up in the rat race, lead unexamined lives, and become cultural (rather than biblical) Christians.

CHECK OUT THE COLLATERAL DAMAGE

Alone, the men problem is horrific, but the collateral damage on marriages and families is staggering. Tonight, 36 percent of America's seventy-two million children will go to bed in a home without their biological dad. But perhaps the greatest cost to the *physical* absence of fathers is the *practical* absence of mothers. Essentially, one person must now do the work of two. As a young woman who grew up without a dad said, "When my mom and dad divorced, I didn't just lose my dad. I also lost my mom, because she had to work long hours to support us."

- Of men who married between 1970 and 1974, just 46.2 percent were still married after thirty years.[5]
- 48 percent of women are choosing cohabitation over marriage.[6]
- 41 percent of babies are born to single mothers.[7]
- 36 percent of children live in homes without their biological fathers.[8]
- 18 percent of pregnancies are terminated by abortion.[9]

- Children in female-headed families are five times more likely to live in poverty, repeat a grade, and have emotional problems compared to families where a father is present.[10]

We have become a nation of *spiritual* widows and *practical* orphans (James 1:27). These are real people—real casualties. For example, my father-in-law and I have lunch once a week. One Monday our waitress, Abby (name changed), seemed a little down, so I struck up a conversation.

She told us the parking lot in front of the restaurant had flooded during a torrential Florida storm the day before, and now her car wouldn't start. She had tears in her eyes, so I knew there had to be more to the story.

I guessed she was so overwhelmed by what for most of us would be a small inconvenience because she didn't have much money. I told her how sorry we were, and that we would say a prayer for her when we prayed over lunch.

Then I asked her a few more questions. She was twenty-six years old, a single mom with six- and eight-year-old boys, and had no family in Orlando. The father of her children wasn't in the picture anymore, so she was left to raise two sons without a father figure by working for tips.

Her mother died when she was fourteen and her younger brother was eight years old. Their father did not step up. Perhaps he didn't know how, but he still failed them. She had made some bad choices, but now was trying to do the right thing for her two sons. Yet it worried her that they had no positive male influence.

After she brought our food, she started walking away. On impulse, I called her back and invited her to join us as we prayed; she did, and I sensed that God encouraged her heart.

Then she went on to say that she was deeply worried about her younger brother, now twenty, who, without a positive father figure, was on the cusp of making some poor life decisions as well. So I told her about the work we do with men and gave her a copy of *The Man in the Mirror* for him.

It's an all too familiar pattern, isn't it? Abby has five men in her life. Her father? A poor male example. The father of her children? Another poor example. Her brother? Which way will he go? Her two sons? What will become of them?

What a perfect example of why God wants us to disciple men. Experiences like this are why we can never, and will never, tire or lose our passion for evangelizing and discipling men. The mission of "men's discipleship" is for all of the broken people, like Abby and her sons, left in the wake of misguided men. Those men have no idea of the destructive forces they are setting in motion that will devastate multiple generations.

As a police officer once said, "Statistics are tragedies with the tears wiped away."

IT'S A CHRISTIAN PROBLEM, TOO

There's more. We also have a *Christian* "men problem" with devastating results. As I wrote in my book *Man Alive*, I'd estimate that as many as 90 percent of Christian men lead lukewarm, stagnant, often defeated lives. They're mired in spiritual mediocrity—and they hate it.

Despite their good intentions, after they "walk the aisle" and "pray the sinner's prayer," most men return to their seats and resume their former lives. They don't take the next steps. Almost imperceptibly, one disappointment at a time, the world sucks out their newfound joy and passion for life in Christ.

Men lose heart, go silent, and anesthetize their pain. Then they give up, burn out, drop out, or just slowly drift away. ***It's not just getting older; it's an assassination of the soul.***

And isn't that exactly what the enemy of our souls wants? As Jesus said, referring to the devil, "The thief comes to steal and kill and destroy" (John 10:10).

Today's average man is like a deer caught in the headlights of a Humvee. He doesn't fully understand—and so can't apply—what God has to say about a man's identity, purpose, relationships, marriage, sex, fathering, work, money, ministry, time, emotions, integrity, and dozens of other subjects.

As a result, most men are tired. They often have a lingering feeling something isn't quite right about their lives. Often their lives are coming unglued. And it is common for them to feel like nobody really cares. Even in the church, men are being left behind. The situation is so significant that in the next chapter we will explore this in depth.

Yet men routinely "bluff" when asked, "How are you doing?" Pastors observe this all the time. For that reason, I think we should be just as concerned about the men who have not become statistics as those who have.

No man fails on purpose. None of us wakes up in the morning and thinks, *I wonder what I can do today to irritate my wife, neglect my kids, work too much, let my walk with God lapse, or have a moral failure.* But many of us will. And that, in a nutshell, is the "men problem." And it is screaming for an immediate solution.

THE OPPORTUNITY

Reaching these men is one of the great strategic opportunities—and needs—of our time. **In this book I'm going to bring you up to date on what works with men, what doesn't work, and why it matters now more than ever.**

Instead of the "men problem," some quarters need to start seeing the "men opportunity." Pastors are the logical choice. Pastors bring grace to the equation. They see men not so much for what they are, but for what they can become in Christ. Pastors are the ones whom God has called to instruct, encourage, correct, challenge, inspire, and call men to "act like a man." This is a significant yet solvable problem. There is no human or spiritual reason why we can't get this done. Of course, "it" will take time and dedication.

The purpose of this book is to equip you to more effectively pastor *all* of your men. God's vision is that *every* man in your church becomes a disciple of Jesus. Men's ministry needs to be redefined so that it is "all-inclusive." However our men got in so deep, can you think of any other solution than to disciple them out? *This is a book about why and how to disciple every man in your church.*

You'll learn an *intentional process* that can help you disciple every "willing" man in your church to find Christ, grow in his faith, and serve the Lord. And I'm going to show you how to build a *sustainable ministry* that will . . .

- Increase the number of men in your church
- Inspire men to populate your new and existing spiritual growth groups and classes
- Encourage men to serve in your new and existing ministry opportunities
- Surface men who can become leaders for your church

For example, a friend of mine started a small group with seven men in his Birmingham, Alabama, church. During the next seven years, his ministry grew to seven groups totaling 128 men. At that time his church needed about 150 leaders to function properly. One hundred of those leaders came through his small groups. But what's especially intriguing is that approximately seventy-five of those men—fully half of the church's leadership!—started in his groups as cultural Christians who would (probably) not have otherwise stepped up to become church leaders.

You would not be holding this book in your hands unless pastoring men was important to you. But if I were to ask you, "Are you effective in pastoring your men?" like most pastors you would very likely say, "No." I've discovered that even pastors who rank among the most successful at pastoring their men are hesitant to say, "Yes, I'm effective."

When asked why he was so tentative, one successful pastor said, "I know too much. I know that even though we've made progress with a man by taking him through our basic discipleship course, then officer training, and now he's a leader—I still see areas in his life that need work—as in my own, or I hear about someone who had a negative experience with him and I say to myself, 'Hmmm, he's not quite there.'"

Most church leaders we talk to are profoundly dissatisfied with the number of men in their churches who are effective disciples. But the majority of churches that have tried to implement men's discipleship initiatives have not been able to sustain them. They need better information, models, methods, and processes grounded in research, field testing, and biblical authority. That's why I wrote this book.

This is not a book about how to get a men's group going in your church. This is not a book about changing the décor of your sanctuary. This is not a book about starting a "separate" men's ministry that reaches a fraction of your men. Those are secondary concerns.

Since 1973 I have been "pastoring men," and here are three promises I want to make. By the end of this book you will know:

- *The state of your men*—how they are doing, what they want, what keeps them from getting what they want, and what they need (chapters 2–5)
- *The essential factors* to successfully disciple men (chapters 7 and 8)
- *A concrete, sustainable strategy* to help you organize your passion for men's discipleship without a lot of new programming. As you will see, you are probably already doing most of what needs to be done (chapter 9)

WHY I CARE SO MUCH ABOUT YOU AND YOUR MEN

Helping pastors disciple their men is my passion for personal reasons. In 1926, when my dad was two, the youngest of four children, his father deserted his family.

The stress got the best of my grandmother. She had a stroke, so she and her four young children moved in with two of her unmarried sisters (my great-aunts). Together, those three women raised my dad and his siblings. They did a great job, but they were dirt poor.

In those days, long before government programs, the community closed ranks when some of "their people" were in need. The one sister who worked was an elevator operator at the local bank. Knowing the situation, the employer paid her a generous salary of $50 a week (roughly $15 an hour in today's dollars). She bought groceries each day on her way home. The grocer told her, "Nina, you take whatever you need, and pay whatever you can."

When my dad turned six, he went to work with his older brother, Harry. They had two jobs. They rose every morning at 3:00 a.m. to deliver milk and then worked a paper route. The school gave them a permanent tardy slip.

My dad never knew the warmth of a father's embrace. He never felt the scratch of a dad's whiskers. He never overheard his dad whistling or singing while he worked, never smelled his work clothes, never heard him joke around or read a bedtime story, never tossed a ball, never felt a dad tussle his hair, never heard him say, "I love you, son" or "I'm proud of you, son," and never had a father's approval or guidance.

When Dad became a man, he had to decide if he would repeat or break the cycle. As the oldest of four boys, I'm grateful my dad wanted to break the cycle. But fathering was unexampled to him. So our family joined a church because Dad and Mom wanted to get some moral and religious instruction for their four sons. Like many people, they believed the church would be the one place in the world where they could turn for help.

Our church had a vision to put my dad to work and, because of his strong work ethic, he responded to the challenge. By age forty, my dad was the top layman in the church. I suppose that's what he thought it meant to be a "good Christian."

Of course, there is a lot of work to do in the church, but our church did not also have a vision to disciple my dad to be a godly man, father, and husband—the real reason he joined. He did the best he could, but he was left to "guess" at how to father my brothers and me.

Something happened in the church that hurt my mother's feelings, and my dad was burned out, so we quit church when I was in the tenth grade and my youngest brother was in the third grade.

Our family was soon hit by a force from which we have still not fully recovered. I quit high school in the middle of my senior year. My brother Robert followed in my footsteps. He eventually died of a heroin overdose. My other two brothers have had a variety of employment, substance, and marriage issues.

My dad just never saw it coming. If he could have seen around the bend of that decision, I'm sure he would have done things differently. If he was still alive I know he would say, "I take full responsibility. That was my decision." And I respect that. Every man does need to take responsibility for his own life. Don't you wish more men would?

But I would like to suggest that the church is culpable. The church knew (or should have known) what was around the bend. The church should have had a vision to disciple my Dad. But it didn't.

Fortunately, God is the Redeemer, and this story took another turn—I fell in love with Patsy. She went forward at a Billy Graham Crusade to publicly profess her faith at the age of eleven, and has never wavered. God graciously grafted the gospel back into my family line through Patsy's family line—Patsy led me to Christ.

Then God allowed me the joy of leading my brother Robert to Christ before he died. Another brother has also professed Christ, and so has my only niece on this side of the family. Dad and Mom also both came to Christ (or came back—I'm not sure). Neither one of them ever got over their bitterness toward the church, but they both affirmed their faith in Jesus on their deathbeds.

Both of my children grew up loving Christ. My Dad and I had the same DNA, so what was the difference? Why did I succeed where he failed? The difference was that I belonged to a church that had a vision to disciple me to be a godly man, husband, and father, while my Dad did not.

When I walked through the front door of that church, there were men who were ready for me, and other men like me. They had sat around a table and pondered, "Why would he do that? Why would a man walk through our front door? What is the problem he's trying to solve?" Those men took me under their wings and showed me the ropes. And our pastor was behind it all the way.

Church is where I learned how to study the Bible for myself, how to study together with others, and how to share my faith and lead someone to Christ. In other words, church is where I became a disciple and disciple-maker. Where else could that happen?

The reason I am so passionate about equipping pastors and churches to disciple men is this: I know that in every church there are men just like my Dad. These are men with good hearts and good intentions who have come to church for all the right reasons. How tragic when they fall away.

I also believe that in most churches there are men like my grandfather—men who are not only going to pull the plug on church, but on their families too. And they have no idea of the forces of destruction they're about to set in motion— that a century later, like me, their children's children may still be trying to recover from that fateful decision.

At the Man in the Mirror ministry, we see it every day in the broken homes and shattered lives of families who have lost a husband, father, and provider.

Obviously I will never know what it might have been like to grow up in a family with a dad who was discipled to be a godly man, husband, and father. My hope and prayer is that by learning and applying the skills in this book, you will feel equipped to more effectively pastor men like my dad and the grandfather I never knew—and men like me who sincerely want to break the cycle but can't do it without your help. May the young boys growing up in your church today never have to one day repeat a story like mine.

THE ANSWER: THE DISCIPLE-MAKING CHURCH

It's hard to picture solving problems like fatherlessness, divorce, poverty, pornography, racism, homelessness, and Wall Street corruption—to name a few—isn't it?

But Jesus can do it. Jesus Christ and His gospel is the hope of the world. And we, His body, the church, of whom Christ is head, though deeply flawed and far from perfect, are and always have been God's primary and most effective means of bringing Christ and His gospel to the world.

So this is the question: How do we bring Christ and His gospel to the world in the most effective way? That question has already been answered. Jesus said, "Go and make disciples." He did not post it on Facebook for an opinion poll. See if you agree with this statement. . . .

No matter how we got into the current situation, the only solution is to disciple our way out.

We believe the discipleship opportunity with the most leverage in the world today is to help churches more effectively disciple men.

Why? First, many of the most receptive men already attend church, or are hanging around the fringe. As D. L. Moody said, "I would rather wake a slumbering church than a slumbering world." Why did he say that? Again, it's about leverage.

Second, men are pacesetters. When men become disciples of Jesus, that discipleship percolates into their marriages, families, workplaces, communities, Facebook posts, gym conversations, and the world. Again, leverage.

Can you picture ever getting your community right without first getting your churches right? Not very likely, is it?

Can you picture ever getting your churches right without getting families right? Probably not going to happen, right?

Can you picture ever getting families right without getting marriages right? That's straight out of family systems theory 101.

And can you picture ever getting marriages right without getting men right? That's just not going to happen, wouldn't you agree?

It really is about the men. And virtually every church has a "men problem."

Scientists keep looking for a holy grail that unifies the cosmos—a "theory of everything." Pastors don't have to keep looking. We have a unifying theory. Jesus taught us the holy grail for unifying His church: it's making disciples. Discipleship is the core mission Jesus gave His bride.

Making disciples is God's designated way to release the power of His gospel on every problem your men face. It's the irrefutable biblical mission of your church.

Discipleship is how men become civilized. The institutional church is God's appointed means—the "first responders"—to help men become disciples. However, the church (in general) has not been making disciples at a proper pace. According to one survey, only 16 percent of church-attending adults are involved in organized discipleship classes, and twice as many women as men. (Discipleship, of course, is a lot more than attending classes; we will examine discipleship closely in chapters 5 and 6.)

One day a highly placed executive in one of America's largest evangelical denominations told me, "In our denomination, we are not making disciples. And that's because our pastors have never been discipled."

Later, my wife and I went to dinner with the chancellor of a seminary and his wife. I told him what the denominational leader (from a different denomination) had said. He lamented, "Well, I'm not surprised. We find that when our students arrive, they have never been discipled. And we have no plans to disciple them while they're here." (He later initiated a pilot program with full-time staffing to disciple their students.)

So people who have never been discipled go to seminary where they are not discipled, and then they are sent to churches where their main responsibility is to—what? Make disciples.

Talk about an elephant in the living room! As a result, many pastors feel ill-equipped to disciple their men. They don't feel like they understand what their men are going through or how to help them. The unhappy result is that men don't get what they need from their church, and the church doesn't get what it needs from its men. That's why I wrote this book—to give you the confidence and tools you need to disciple your men.

If you project out twenty or fifty years, can you visualize any way of ever getting the world right if men are wrong? The "men problem" is the root cause behind virtually every problem that ails us. It's an untreated cancer that keeps producing more and worse tumors.

One day a major donor said, "Pat, I can't support your ministry anymore."

I said, "That's fine, but tell me why."

He said, "My heart is really in prison ministry and teenage crisis pregnancy centers."

I laughed out loud. I said, "By all means please support that important work. But why do you think so many young men end up in prison? And why do you think a young teenaged girl would hop into bed with a boy?" (We dialogued more and he did continue his support.)

Let's treat the symptoms, of course, but let those who can—pastors—also treat the disease. A disciple-making church offers the only *systemic* solution to what ails us.

We need a fresh, research-based, pastor-led, biblical, field-tested approach that results in lasting change—one that is "actionable."

WE NEED A FRESH APPROACH

There have always been men's movements. The contemporary secular and Christian men's movements both started circa 1990. The secular men's movement went "blip" and promptly disappeared.

The problem with the secular men's movement was that it had no answer for "Tuesday." Men were lured into the woods on Saturday where they painted themselves up like Indians, beat on tom-toms, talked to trees, and cried out in existential pain. By Sunday they felt relief. But on Monday they had to return to civilization, and by Tuesday the futility and pain had returned.

The contemporary Christian men's movement has survived because Jesus Christ prevails on Tuesday. Instead of war paint, whoops, and grunts, men are being discipled into the gospel of Jesus. By the late 1990s, the nexus of the movement had shifted from loud stadiums into the quiet corridors of the local church.

Yet by the early part of this century, the Christian men's movement could be characterized as "a lot of men with really good hearts doing the best they could." There had been a lot of false starts.

Many pastors and laymen had devoted as many as ten years to untested strategies that really were doomed to fail from the start. And I didn't see any reason to think things would be different in another ten or twenty years—unless we came up with a fresh approach.

WE NEED A RESEARCH-BASED APPROACH

At the same time, I have also sensed the need for a more research-based approach to men's discipleship. So in 2002, to augment my master's in theological studies, I embarked on doctoral research, which led to earning a PhD in management in 2006. For my dissertation I studied the question, "Why do some churches succeed at men's discipleship while others languish or fail?"

My research revolved around two major issues. First, I wanted to learn, "How do church-based men's discipleship ministries that succeed differ from those that languish or fail?" Second, I wanted to discover, "What are successful pastors doing differently than the pastors of ineffective or failed ministries to men?"

I wanted to know from a management perspective, "What are the factors that lead to success or failure when implementing a men's discipleship program?" To get at the answers, I decided on multiple-case-study research. I compared and contrasted churches that had effective men's discipleship programs to churches that had ineffective or failed programs.

We will dive into the deep end of the pool and cover my research findings in chapters 7 and 8, "Success Factors in Discipling Men," but here is the indisputable bottom line: *The senior pastor is the key to everything.* These are the three main factors in the highly effective churches:

1. A senior pastor with the *vision* to disciple every man in the church
2. A senior pastor with the *determination* to succeed
3. A senior pastor who found a *sustainable strategy* to make disciples and disciple-makers

Of course, Jesus is the perfect example of these three factors. In fact, His sustainable strategy has outlasted every institution, organization, kingdom, and government ever established.

When it comes to ministry to men, I am aware of how brutally many over-zealous laymen have treated their pastors. Yet, without you, the pastor, men's discipleship in your church will never be more than a fringe activity. And, as we will see, you can be successful at this without adding a lot of new programming.

WE NEED A PASTOR-LED APPROACH

I cannot overstate this: *No one has more influence with your men than you do.* While writing this book, I was invited to speak to a special men's class at a local church during the Sunday school hour. My speaking was well publicized—both the senior pastor and the executive pastor announced it. About thirty-five men attended, and we had a wonderful time. Simultaneously, the senior pastor was teaching a three-week series for men on Sunday evenings. He had five hundred men attend his men's classes. It was a priority to this pastor, and the men sensed it.

As the pastor, you can accomplish what laymen can only dream about—and so much more quickly. With the support of his senior pastor, John started a small-group ministry in his very busy 1,000-member church in Atlanta. Over the span of seven years, his ministry grew to ten groups with a combined total of about 120 people.

Then a new senior pastor came on board. He shared John's vision for small groups. He convinced the leadership that the congregation should stop coming to the church building on Wednesday nights. Instead, he wanted to break people into small groups that would meet in homes.

In the spring he announced that they would start the new small-group ministry in the fall. Over the summer he preached on the importance and value of small groups. On the first night, 817 people met in small groups.

It took seven *years* for a talented, committed layman (he's in top management with a Fortune 500 company) to recruit 120 people into small groups—even with his pastor's full *support*. With the pastor's *personal involvement*, it took only seven *months* to recruit 817 people into small groups—an increase of nearly 700 percent.

There's no getting around it—the senior pastor is the key to everything.

Everything points to this overarching conclusion: For a critical mass of men to become disciples in a church, pastors will need to take the lead. To succeed you will need biblically sound, research-based, field-tested strategies and models. It would not be fair to ask you to develop these tools on your own.

WE NEED A BIBLICAL APPROACH

Suppose you wanted to start a company to make computers. You put together a business plan to manufacture 100,000 computers over the next five years. You raise $100 million from an investor.

Five years later your investor returns and asks for a report. You say, "We're doing great! We did it! We produced 100,000 units! We made 15,000 refrigerators, 10,000 toasters, 21,000 microwave ovens, 50,000 lava lamps, and we're up to 4,000 computers!"

Your investor replies, "Wow, 4,000 computers. But that's only 4 percent of what you projected."

"Oh yes," you say, "but look at all the other useful things we've produced!"

"That's wonderful," he says, "but I was planning to use those computers to change the world. Now it can't happen. You've made the world more comfortable. I wanted to make it different."

For 2,000 years we (the church) have only had one business plan: "Go and make disciples" (Matthew 28:19). The final marching orders from Jesus are "Go and make disciples." Those orders still stand. They have not been amended, altered, or rescinded. More millions of people and more billions of dollars have been mobilized by this brief message than any other speech in recorded history.

Our "investor," Jesus, could have directed us to make anything He wanted. He could have said, "Go and make *worshipers*." But He didn't. He said, "Go and make disciples."

He could have said, "Go and make *workers*." But He didn't. He said, "Go and make disciples."

He could have said, "Go and make *tithers*." But He didn't. He said, "Go and make disciples."

Does that mean Jesus isn't interested in worshipers, workers, and tithers? Of course He is. But Jesus knew we wouldn't get worshipers by trying to make worshipers. Making worshipers can be little more than teaching people how to sing. No, we get worshipers by making disciples. Because how would people be able to worship a God they do not know?

Jesus also knew we wouldn't get workers by trying to make workers, tithers by trying to make tithers, and so on. But everything falls into place when we make disciples. True disciples can't wait to work and worship and tithe (and serve, do acts of mercy, evangelize, love one another, and so on).

The central mission of the church—the overarching goal—is to "make disciples." Discipleship is the "portal" priority through which all the other desired outcomes of the *ecclesia* are achieved. (The "portal" priority concept is explained graphically in chapter 9.) The key to success at every point is, "Go and make disciples." The pastor's chief role is to make disciples.

There is one, and only one, way in which a man can win the battle for his soul. It is simple and concrete. His single greatest need is to become a disciple of our Lord and Savior, Jesus Christ. To be a disciple of Jesus is the highest honor to which a man can aspire. The goal of pastoring men, then, is to disciple men into the gospel.

WE NEED A FIELD-TESTED APPROACH

What I'm presenting in this book has been learned and practiced in the field. It's not theoretical. My personal mission is to help men grow as disciples and disciple-makers—starting at home. A large part of my purpose and calling—and also for Man in the Mirror, the ministry I founded in 1991—is to help bring vision, strategic thinking, and organization to the Christian men's discipleship movement.

I am a men's specialist—a "one-trick" pony—a consultant on men's issues, and an advocate for men. So are the individuals on the large field staff of Man in the Mirror who consult with churches in all fifty states to help them disciple men more effectively. Our vision is "for every church to disciple every man."

While I do have a seminary degree, God did not call me to become ordained. Instead, God's clear calling on my life has been to serve pastors by helping them reach and build men. From the time I became a Christian in 1973, my overarching passion has been to challenge men to stop, examine their lives, be reconciled to Christ, and make needed changes based on God's greater purposes for their lives.

Since 1986 I have taught a new Bible message (almost) every week to the estimated 15,000 men who attend The Man in the Mirror Bible Study—150 men who meet every Friday morning at a local civic center and the rest online.

The Man in the Mirror Bible Study is now downloaded thousands of times each week—many of those for men's groups that meet in churches, conference rooms, and cubicles around the world. I figure I've prepared and delivered over 1,250 different messages tailored specifically to men.

When I wrote *The Man in the Mirror* in 1989, no one, and least of all me, ever imagined the millions of men God would touch through that book! After all, I was an anonymous commercial real estate developer plying my trade here in Central Florida.

In fact, if it weren't for pastors, I wouldn't be in ministry today! In 1989 we had a warehouse full of unsold copies of *The Man in the Mirror*. So we offered them for free to pastors. Seven thousand pastors took up the offer, started quoting from it in sermons, taking elder and deacon groups through it, and that's how the book took off.

And the rest, as they say, is history. I have written twenty books for men and several hundred articles for and about men. In 2000, we started a program to offer books by the case for under $2 each. At this writing, ten million books have been distributed to men through churches. Our faculty members have conducted over a thousand men's seminars in churches throughout the United States and the world.

To date, we have helped 35,000 churches impact 12 million men. Our Leadership Training Center has equipped thousands of churches and leaders in the highly acclaimed No Man Left Behind Model that I will unpack for you in chapter 9, "The No Man Left Behind Model: A Sustainable Strategy to Disciple Every Willing Man in Your Church." Churches throughout the United States are engaging "all" their men using Equip Your Men's Leaders (appendix A), a process we developed for churches to implement the No Man Left Behind principles.

In 2010 we conducted research on the effectiveness of the No Man Left Behind Model. The results seemed too good to be true, so we sent the data off to a university to be verified by PhDs in statistics. We found churches that implemented the No Man Left Behind Model experienced a 48 percent increase in the number of men attending in two and a half years on average; and an 84 percent increase in the number of men involved in discipleship during the same period.

Of course, we immediately realized we had been entrusted with something special to steward. First Corinthians 4:2 says, "Now it is required that those who have been given a trust must prove faithful." So we began asking the question,

"What does faithful look like?"

After much prayer and seeking counsel, we concluded that God wants us to proliferate No Man Left Behind to as many churches as possible throughout America and the world. For that to happen, we are building a field staff who can work with disciple-making pastors and leaders in local communities where they live. We eventually plan to have trained field staff—"boots on the ground"—in every community.

Why am I telling you all this? I tell you these things because I want you to know that I am not writing from an announcer's booth; I am actively in the game, as are you. In this book I consider it my privilege and duty to share with you what we have learned through these field-tested experiences.

Research-based, field-tested concepts are important so you don't waste your time—often measured in years—on plans and programs based on untested theories, strong opinions, or good intentions. For example, a lot of thinkers have tried to turn the church's failures with men into a gender issue. They offer solutions that address making the church more male friendly. I'm certainly not against this, but it falls in the category of "second things." It's just a theory, and one that may prove costly. As my dissertation committee often asked me, "Sez who?"

If you're not careful, you can end up with a committee talking incessantly about decorating themes instead of how to lead men into a vital communion with the living Christ. I'm almost embarrassed to write those two concepts in the same sentence.

I don't think Jesus minds if your church wants to park a Harley in the narthex—it's not the main thing, but neither is it prohibited (and it's probably a culturally relevant idea). But I do think Jesus desperately cares if your church wants to disciple men into His gospel, equip them to disciple others, and help them become friends of God.

It takes a long time to make a disciple, the process is often messy, and it rarely proceeds in a "step-by-step" sequence. To illustrate, I've included a case study of how I became a disciple in chapter 6.

In Appendix B, "Why the Man in the Mirror Men's Bible Study Works—A Case Study," I will break down for you what I think makes this long-running, field-tested Bible study an effective model for men's discipleship—as well as share with you the major challenges we've had to overcome.

WHAT HAPPENS WHEN A MAN
BECOMES A DISCIPLE?

As the pastor, you hear a loud knock on your door. It's Jason Steele—a "Sunday only" Christian for seventeen years. But three years ago you decided that discipling men needed to be one of your top priorities. Two years ago, your church sponsored a seminar to create momentum among men on the fringe, and Jason attended. Though it wasn't anything you hadn't said all along, the speaker came at things from a different angle, and the message rang Jason's bell. (Actually, the only reason an outside speaker can harvest is that you have faithfully prepared the soil. See John 4:36–38.)

Jason surrendered his life to Christ at that point—whether for the first time or as a recommitment, it's hard to say.

When offered a six-week, follow-up discussion group, Jason leaped at the chance to sign up. At the end of the six weeks, the leader asked him for "six more weeks" to go a little deeper. Eventually, the group gelled into a long-term Bible study and prayer group.

Jason, like many men in your church, has come to know and love Christ with a passion. And now here he is, standing in your doorway. He says, "Pastor, you have to give me something to do—a work or service or ministry of some kind. As I have grown to understand more about the unfathomable work of the cross, I can no longer sit idle. I can no longer be happy unless I do something to serve this great God. What can I do to help you?"

This is a great day in your life. Even though the results seemed small at first, you persevered with "discipling men" as a top priority. The long hours of building into the lives of your men, the countless prayers for God to send workers, your determination—at this moment all of it seems worth the effort.

Soon after Jason, other men begin to trickle, then flood, into your office. At the five-year mark, you actually run out of ministries for men inside the church! Now you start "sending" workers into community-based ministries.

One day the financial secretary brings you a report that the church has a surplus. As the men have grasped their roles as stewards, they have been much more generous. Gone is the need to plead for finances. You have been able to respond to additional requests from missionaries for support that you once had to turn away.

One afternoon your secretary announces at 3:00 p.m. that all your marriage counseling appointments for the day are finished.

"What?" you say, in a mild state of shock. As your men have come to understand their duty to love and nurture their wives, marriages have been healed and the counseling load has dwindled. On that happy day, you arrive home early and have a meaningful conversation with your own wife!

Then one day, your youth minister brings you a report that the youth facilities are out of space. Apparently, as the young people have watched their fathers transformed before their very eyes, they want in on what's happening. They have flocked to the youth meetings to learn more about this Jesus, this radical person who changed their fathers' lives.

More men. Growing men. More workers. Better leaders. Bigger budgets. Restored marriages. Curious youth. A balanced workload. A strong reputation in the community. An increase in first-time visitors. Spiritual satisfaction. A calling come true.

Sound too good to be true? There are churches all over America experiencing these results because the pastor has focused on discipling men.

IS PASTORING MEN WORTH THE EFFORT?

There is raging in the cosmos and all around us a titanic battle between the forces of good and evil for men's souls. This battle is raging out of control in neighborhoods across America—your neighborhood. Sound overstated?

Think for a moment about the casualties taking place on your street, where your men work, even in your church. Men leave homes, women weep, a little twelve-year-old girl prays, "God, why is my daddy always so angry?"

This is a real battle. These are real men with real families.

I love the church, but the church on the whole has not been able to muster an ongoing will or comprehensive strategy to disciple men. Pastoring men is not a top priority in *any* denomination based upon their actual allocations of financial and intellectual resources.

Nevertheless, we should be optimistic. Together, we can create a national dialogue about the importance of reaching men—men like my dad, my grandfather, and me. I thank God all the time for inserting me into a disciple-making church. In fact, I shudder at the thought of what might have been.

This is a battle worth fighting. Woodrow Wilson said, "I would rather fail in a cause that will ultimately succeed than succeed in a cause that will ultimately fail."

This is also a battle we can win. The challenge before us is daunting, but not impossible. In fact, Jesus Christ will win. We cannot, we must not, and, by God's grace, we will not fail. Pastoring men is worth the effort.

Ultimately, though, we need to pastor men because it's the right thing to do. Pastoring men may not be easy or glamorous, and it's often thankless work. Yet when a man conquers his "men problem," that will likely change the entire course of his family for many generations to come.

And what if you're behind? A Chinese proverb says, "The best time to plant a tree was twenty years ago. The second best time is now."

So where should we start? Before we work on the solution, let's make sure we're clear about the "men problem"—how are men doing, what do they want, and what keeps them from getting what they want?

PART 1

UNDERSTAND YOUR MEN

HOW ARE YOUR MEN DOING?

When historians write the "cultural autopsy" for our generation, what will they say? A lot will depend on how well the church responds to the needs of men today. To give men what they need, we must first understand how they are doing.

Demographically, men are quite different. They are black, white, Hispanic, rich, poor, rural, suburban, urban, trade workers, professionals, conservative, liberal, short, tall, skinny, fat, bald, gray, young, old, bright, and not so bright. Some like to ponder their next chess move; others prefer screaming over a touchdown with 70,000 of their closest friends.

For every man who sits on a board at a company, another lies on a bunk in jail. In his book *Is There Anything Good About Men?* scholar Roy Baumeister has made a strong case that men are given to extremes. Just as there are more men who are millionaires than women, so are there more men in prison than women.[1]

In another sense, all men are quite similar. Each man's wiring diagram is not so different from any other of the male gender. Whether I am speaking with men from Alabama or Alaska, at the Pentagon or in prison, executives in New York City or Mennonite farmers in Pennsylvania, cowboys in Texas or Chinese businessmen in Malaysia, I have found that, as men, our similarities dwarf our differences.

In the previous chapter we looked at some of the numbing statistics about men and the havoc they've created. You no doubt can add a few favorite stats of your own. Instead of wading deeper into stats, in chapters 2 through 4 I want to give you a psychographic profile of men. This profile fits almost all men, especially men in the workforce. Also, it makes no difference whether you have a small church or a big church, a rural church or an urban church, a charismatic church or a mainline church, or whether your congregation includes upper-income executives or farmers—these similarities among men transcend demographic profiling.

For example, a pastor wrote me and said, "Over 70 percent of my men are in farming and ranching. If I say something to them about my view of debt, their response is, 'Yeah, but you were never in farming. You can't make it in this business without large loans and taking on debt.'

"Some of my men are under almost unbelievable financial stress. Hail, drought, and harsh weather have made this year especially disappointing. One of my best men was advised by his lawyer a year ago to declare bankruptcy, which he didn't do. 'I'm looking to lose $50,000 this year,' he told me last Sunday. He is really under pressure and is working his tail off! Scarce is time for his precious wife and two teenaged children."

You could easily substitute "manufacturing" or "software" for "farming" and "ranching," and nothing else would change. So, yes, these are generalizations, but the pattern is pretty close.

A MAN'S INTENTIONS

A man is a noble creature. After all, it's men who insist, "Women and children in the lifeboats first." Men are famous for making heroic sacrifices. By nature, men lead, protect, and provide for their families and fight for justice.

The doctrine of total depravity notwithstanding, most men have it in their hearts to do the right thing. Most men are trying to earn an honest living, be loving husbands, good dads, contributing citizens, and, if religious, solid churchmen.

Of course, men often do fail, but I don't think anyone would suggest they fail on purpose. This conflict between "the man I want to be" and "the man I am" is why men show up on Sunday morning. Men come to church because, like my Dad and later like me, they are looking for some help. Many of your men could easily write the following letter on a Sunday morning and slip it in your hand after the service. It's what they are going through.

Dear Pastor,

As I was sitting in church on Sunday, I decided to write you this letter. When the service began, this is what I found myself thinking . . .

I'm here, pastor, I'm here. I worked 55 hours this week (that's five days from 8 to 6 and two hours every night after the kids went to bed), slept 48 hours (I'm short one whole night), spent Saturday morning shuttling between soccer games, worked Saturday afternoon on the yard, took my wife to dinner Saturday night, and now here I am on Sunday morning.

All week long the world has told me to buy everything from computers to cars, and to want everything from more sex to more fun. My boss is not happy with me, nor I with him. My spouse appreciates my problems, but she has problems of her own. She's frustrated that I don't spend enough time with the family, but doesn't complain about the money. Besides, I can't share many of my struggles with her—like sexual temptations, work overload, and how to cover all these bills. The kids need more of me, but it's not like they can really tell the difference—I've always shorted them.

Meanwhile, I read my Bible and prayed four mornings this week—a total of one hour. I don't wake up in the morning wanting to fail. My intentions are good, but I still fall short. I've come here to receive some encouragement and direction from God. Now, what do you want me to do? What can you say to me?

With great appreciation for all you do as our pastor,
Jim

It's hard to solve a problem we don't really understand. We already know that a lot of men are not right, right? But before we try to "fix" the problem, let's slow down and try to understand what is really going on. How are men doing—really? The following profile applies to all men who have not been equipped as disciples, and sometimes even if they have.

HOW ARE MEN DOING? A PSYCHOGRAPHIC PROFILE
Men Are Tired

First, most men are tired. Since I work with men as a vocation, sometimes I'm asked, "If you could only make one observation about how men are doing, what would it be?" This is it: If there is one thing you can know for sure about your men, it's that they're tired. And not just physically tired—although that too— but mentally, emotionally, relationally, morally, and financially tired. They are exhausted from the fast pace of our demanding, me, now, instant, online, real-time culture. You know the words that get tossed around: *stressed, slammed, weary, in need of relief, wasted, fragile, short-fused.* These are all synonyms that add up to "tired."

The average Christian male is up to his neck in debts and duties. He has a "picture" in his mind of what it means to be a "good Christian." He believes in this picture—it's what he thinks he "needs" to do to be a "good boy"—to be happy. He often measures his spirituality by whether or not he can live up to these standards. They are, after all, good ideas. But they are not the gospel.

- I need to spend quality time with my wife.
- I need to be a super dad to my kids and attend (maybe coach) all their activities. My dad did (or didn't) do this for me, and I'm going to be there for them.
- I need to make lots of money so my family can live in a beautiful home in a "better" neighborhood, my kids can wear the right labels, there is less pressure on my wife to work, and I can become financially independent.
- I need to join a men's small group where I can grow with some brothers.
- I need to attend a weekly home-growth and fellowship group.
- I need to have a daily quiet time for fellowship with God.
- I need to keep the Sabbath and have my family in church to worship God.
- I need to serve God through a personal ministry—probably through the church.
- I need to be a good citizen and neighbor.
- I need to be a star at work if all this is going to happen.
- I need a successful and satisfying career.
- I need some time for myself.

And now *I'm* tired! Just reading the list is a bit overwhelming. Of course, this is a crooked, performance-based view of faith.

Your men are tired. As a result, most of them are in a "structural hurry." Hurry is structured into a man's schedule. For many men, the car that was once a sanctuary has become a mobile office. They're constantly on their mobile phone trying to wrap up a sale as they navigate to the Little League fields to prove to themselves that they are "okay" as Christian men. One man told me he speeds to work to "save time."

The price of pace is peace. The forced, steady application of the will to make things happen leads to weariness.

Of course, it's not just your men. I suspect that you are probably a little tired too.

No wonder men wince when you ask them to do something. No wonder men plop down in front of the television to vegetate instead of reading a book or having a conversation with their wives. No wonder, no wonder, no wonder. We have created a culture that requires more energy than men have to give. Sometimes we call this the rat race.

They Feel Something Isn't Right

As noted in chapter 1, *men often have a lingering feeling that something isn't quite right about their lives.* This is the second element of our psychographic profile, and it's the inevitable result of running the rat race. A woman told me she was having difficulty figuring out how to offer support to her husband. He loves his work. Occasionally, for stretches of months at a time, he will work twelve-hour days. Then suddenly his mood will swing, and he will mope around for months. When she asks him what it is he wants, he cannot articulate an answer. Something isn't right about his life, but he's not sure what it is.

"I can chart these cycles on paper," she told me. "They're completely predictable. I just don't know what to do for him anymore. He is extremely successful. He has the job he always wanted. We have a beautiful home and two lovely children. What's his problem?"

It does beg the question: How can a man get exactly what he wants and still not be happy?

Their Plans Aren't Working

Third, men's lives are not turning out as they had planned. Each week, on average, four new men visit the live location of the Man in the Mirror Bible study I teach here in Orlando. Our average visitor is typically friendless, overextended in most areas, has at least seen his Bathsheba, is up to his eardrums in debt, lacks meaning and purpose, feels he is under a lot of pressure, and is generally miserable. All of this is carefully masked behind a game face because the man knows that if the sharks smell blood, it's over.

Many of these men have made a profession of faith in Christ, but they have not been trained (discipled) to integrate their faith into their daily lives. They are like men who enlisted in the army and were issued a rifle that they'd never learned how to clean and shoot. As Denzel Washington, playing a recovering alcoholic ex-military bodyguard in a Latin American country, said in *Man on Fire*, "You're either trained or you're not trained." Spiritually, most men are not. Evangelism without discipleship is cruel.

It's not as though these men want to struggle or fail. But their *capabilities* are not equal to their *intentions*. As a result, they get caught up in the rat race—the conflict between who they are created to be and who they are tempted to be. When they lead unexamined lives, these men tend to be Christian in spirit, but secular in practice. Many become cultural Christians who love this life more than the next. They have almost always become lukewarm in faith, worldly in behavior, and hypocritical in witness. Let's give them some credit, though; they come to church because they sense the need for a spiritual solution.

They Feel "Unglued"

Fourth, a lot of men feel like their lives are coming unglued. The problem is not that men are failing to meet their goals. In most cases, they *are* meeting them. The problem, it turns out—they're the wrong goals. A man in his thirties explained, "When I got out of school, I made out a list of everything I thought I would need to be happy. Fifteen years later I have everything on my list. Now I realize . . . it's the wrong list."

How does a man give his best years to a system that never had any possibility of satisfying the hunger of his soul?

They Feel Nobody Cares

Fifth, most men feel like nobody, with the possible exception of family, really cares about them personally. A pastor invited one of his businessmen—a prominent one—to lunch one day. The man took the pastor to his private club. After forty-five minutes of eating and exchanging social pleasantries, they finished their meal. The man set down his napkin and said, "So tell me. What's on your mind? What can I do for you today?"

The pastor said, "Nothing, really. I just wanted to spend some time with you and get to know you better as a person."

"Well, there must be something I can do for you."

"No, not really."

"Are you sure? How are our finances?"

"No, really. I just wanted to get to know you better—man to man."

Two or three more similar exchanges took place.

The man sat there incredulous. Belief slowly crept across his face, and tears welled up in his eyes. He struggled to maintain control of himself. A minute went by. The man regained his composure and said, "In my entire career, no one has ever asked me to lunch unless they wanted something from me."

They're Committed to Values, Not Christ

Sixth, many men are committed to a set of Christian values but not to Christ. At lunch one day, I asked Ron to tell me about his Christian experience. He waxed eloquent about chairing a pastor relations committee and teaching Sunday school. But after ten minutes, he had still made no mention of Christ. It was clear that Ron was not giving a clear testimony of faith and repentance. I asked a follow-up. No progress. Another question. Same conclusion.

Suddenly it dawned on me, *He doesn't know the Lord!* Ron was a pillar in the community and in the church—but not a believer! Then I shared my story. I told him how I had been committed to *a set of Christian values,* but not to *faith in Jesus.* When I told him that Christianity is not about having the *correct information* or even the *correct behavior* but a *correct relationship* with God through Jesus, he became visibly shaken. Through an exchange of emails over the next several hours, he surrendered his life to Christ in faith and repentance.

They're Disappointed with God

Seventh, most men only know enough about God to be disappointed with Him. Bill made a profession of faith at an early age, but thought Christianity was just a bunch of rules that he soon concluded he could not keep. He never really took *possession* of his *profession.*

He started bluffing his way through life as though he really had it all together. Actually, he did have his own morality well within his grasp. By his late thirties, "life" wasn't working, but he was trapped by the pretensions of his own bluff. One day he said, "I feel like I'm a 1,000 piece puzzle with ten pieces missing. I don't know what they are, or where to find them."

They listen to your sermons, they try to do the right things, they have it in their hearts to be faithful Christians, but they don't have much joy, and certainly lack victory over sinful habits. They feel a sense of shame. That's because—whether offered to them or not—they have not become disciples.

It's really not your fault. Men are responsible for their own actions. You do, however, hold the key to helping them get on, or back on, course.

They're Apathetic about Church

Eighth, most men don't think the church is addressing their real-life problems. In addition to a "men problem," we also have a "church problem." They are inextricably linked. I hope it's different in your church, but in many cases men feel like all the church wants is their money, their time, and their families. It may not be fair, but they think of the church as just another performance-oriented organization where they need to step up and make it happen. As a result, most men have a low view of the church. And once a man goes there, he's typically gone—even if he keeps going through the motions.

I'm getting ahead of myself, but this is so important I'll say it here. Jesus, the "head of the body, the church," said, "I will build my church, and [all the powers of hell] will not overcome it" (Matthew 16:18). So teach your men the role and importance of *ecclesia*. Remind them (because they forget) how the church meets the needs of our families: weddings, baptisms, communion, confirmations, funerals, fellowship dinners, evangelistic outreaches, worship services, preaching, hymns, choir, spiritual education, ministry opportunities, accountability, softball leagues, small groups, Sunday school classes, conferences, retreats, nursery, and hospital visits. No institution supports marriage and family like the church.

Remind them what America would look like without the church. Where would be the great hospitals, schools, and universities? Where would be the food pantries, the coalitions for the homeless, the rescue missions? Would anyone be doing inner-city youth work or providing homes for unwed mothers? Where would be the voices calling out for abstinence from premarital sex or the right to life? Who would be the voices of justice and the hands of mercy? Who would be the feet of the gospel of salvation? Who would be the light in the darkness, the salt seeking to preserve society and culture? As someone said, "The church has many critics, but no rivals."

Teach men to be actively involved in church (not merely attend) for the singular reason that the Bible tells us to: "Let us...not [give] up meeting together, as some are in the habit of doing, but [let us encourage] one another—and all the more as you see the Day approaching" (Hebrews 10:24–25). Tell men that the church "assembled" is where they will experience a unique measure of worship, fellowship, growth, service, and accountability. Introduce them to opportunities to become disciples and disciple-makers.

Create an environment where the Holy Spirit can inspire men to engage in life-on-life discipleship. Form them into men's or couples' groups or communities. Keep the groups small enough that men can get to know personally some people who will walk beside them and help them grow and mature in their faith. And inspire them to help others grow and mature in their faith, too.

THE GRACE OF FUTILITY

The situation with men is far from depressing, however. That's because the God of creation is firmly and sovereignly in control. In fact, God is sovereignly and graciously orchestrating all of the seemingly random circumstances of your men. The feeling of futility is the chief tool by which God sovereignly draws men to Himself of their own free will. The apostle Paul explains:

> For the creation was subjected to frustration [futility], not by its own choice, but by the will of the one who subjected it, in hope that the creation itself will be liberated from its bondage to decay and brought into the freedom and glory of the children of God. (Romans 8:20–21)

In other words, God sovereignly introduces futility into the world so that men might come to their senses and be liberated and redeemed.[2] Essentially, He makes life so miserable that your men turn to Him of their own free will.

So why are many Christian men so frustrated? It is exactly because God has set eternity in men's hearts (Ecclesiastes 3:11). They have a built-in sense that life does have meaning, and their frustration is that they have not yet found it. They don't have enough religion to make them happy when they look in the mirror, but they have enough to remind them how unhappy they have become.

Their careers aren't turning out the way they planned or, what's sometimes worse, they are. Their marriages are not working the way they're supposed to, many times their kids don't seem appreciative, and they're up to their receding hairlines in financial problems.

The result? A pervasive lack of contentment stalks them. As Thoreau wrote, "The mass of men lead lives of quiet desperation." They often find themselves frustrated, discouraged, disillusioned, confused, afraid of the future, lonely, and riddled with guilt over poor decisions. They are restless.

They are wondering, "Is this all there is? There must be more to life; there's gotta be." They find their lives are futile—not because they didn't get what they wanted, but because they did. They have met their goals and wonder, "So what?"

Perfect. Such feelings are the grace of God drawing men to Himself. Don't you wish all your men would be that humble and curious?

AN IRONIC REALITY

Of course, there are other types of men in your church. Some are doing great—they're full-fledged disciples and leaders. Others are trapped in destructive cycles. But if you focus on loving and discipling your men as described in this chapter, you will always have more than enough to do.

When a man fails, he sets powerful forces of bondage and brokenness in motion. It can take several generations to break the cycle. As America staggers beneath the load of dozens of major problems—like divorce, fatherlessness, poverty, pornography, adultery, abortion, abuse, disrespect for authority, corruption, ethical failures, and truancy to name a few—where have the men gone? What has happened to our men? At the root of virtually every problem is the failure of a man, ironically a man who got up this morning wishing that his life would make a difference.

These are not bad men. They are, for the most part, men with good intentions. Sinful, yes, but men for whom Christ died. He takes no delight in the death of the wicked. Yet they lack spiritual power. In the next chapter, we will develop a summary of what men want from life.

POINTS TO REMEMBER

- The similarities of men dwarf their differences.
- No man fails on purpose.
- Men are tired.
- Men often have a lingering feeling something isn't quite right about their lives.
- Men's lives are not turning out as they had planned.
- A lot of men feel like their lives are coming unglued.
- Most men feel like nobody, with the possible exception of family, really cares about them personally.
- Many men are committed to a set of Christian values, but not to the person of Christ.
- Most men only know enough about God to be disappointed with Him.
- Most men don't think the church is addressing their real-life problems.
- As a result, their lives feel futile.
- The feeling of futility is the chief tool by which God sovereignly draws men to Himself of their own free will.
- God is sovereignly and graciously orchestrating all of the seemingly random circumstances of your men.

WHAT DO MEN WANT?

We just looked at how men are doing. In this chapter, we'll look at what men want, and in the next chapter, what keeps them from getting what they want.

It's important to remember that Jesus didn't address the Great Commission to the masses. He didn't say, *"Come and be discipled."* Rather, He spoke it to us, His body, the church, and said, *"Go and make disciples."*

If the former, we might be justified talking about telling men what they "need" as our starting point. But because of the very specific way Jesus constructed His marching orders, and to whom, the Great Commission implies a mandate for us to be relevant. To "go" means for us to be with them where they are, not for them to come to us.

So we're wise to start with what men "want" as the basis of our appeal. That's why we have a saying around our office: "Give men what they need in the context of what they want."

In *Man Alive* I wrote that over the last four decades I've met one-on-one with thousands of men over coffee, in restaurants, in offices, online, after Bible studies, or just hanging out at the racetrack. I've listened to their stories. I've heard what they said and didn't say. Christian men know—or strongly sense—that we were created to lead powerful lives transformed by Christ.

But something is blocking them.

With a few inspiring exceptions, most men I talk to are confused about what a powerful, transformed life really looks like, regardless of how much "I love Jesus" they've got. They have high hopes for what Christianity offers but little to show for it.

Their instincts are screaming, *There must be more!*

When men try to put into words what keeps them from feeling fully alive, they invariably describe one or more of these seven symptoms:

- "I just feel like I'm in this thing all alone."
- "I don't feel like God cares about me *personally*—not really."
- "I don't feel like my life has a purpose. It seems random."
- "I have a lot of destructive behaviors that keep dragging me down."
- "My soul feels dry."
- "My most important relationships are not working."
- "I don't feel like I'm doing anything that will make a difference or leave the world a better place."

Do you feel the angst? No doubt you see yourself on this list as well as your men. As you can see, as men, our similarities dwarf our differences.

These inner aches and pains—these yearnings—correspond to the primal, instinctive needs all men share in common.

So what do men want? When I was younger, I had a long list. Over the years I've whittled my list down to three things. I realize that all taxonomies are imperfect summaries, yet when men find *a cause, a companion,* and *a conviction,* everything else generally falls into line. We can summarize it like this:

1. *A cause* we can give our lives to that will make a difference—a mission, significance, meaning, purpose
2. *A companion* to share it with—relationships, love, wife, family, friends, acceptance
3. *A conviction* that gives a reasonable explanation for why numbers 1 and 2 are so difficult—a belief system, worldview, philosophy, religion

This is the essence of manhood—finding *something* we can give ourselves to, *someone* to share it with, and a *system* that explains how to make sense of our lives. These three form the contours of a man's identity and purpose.

Of course, when men find the wrong cause, the wrong woman, or the wrong conviction, everything falls apart, though slowly and rarely detected until the damage has been done.

Notice that we are not yet talking about what men *need*, just what they *want*. Nevertheless, these are God-given desires. That makes them holy, though many men, of course, corrupt them along the way, which is why you and I have a vocation in ministry. An important part of your "pastoring men" skill set is to have a good handle on what men want. Let's delve deeper.

1. A *CAUSE*—SOMETHING WE CAN GIVE OUR LIVES TO

First, men want *something* they can give themselves to that will make a difference. Pounding in the breast of every man is an intense desire to lead a significant life. A man's greatest felt need is his need to be significant—to find meaning and purpose in life, to make a contribution, to discover what he was created by God to do.

Bill, an executive in a major company, was hired because of his accomplishments and extraordinary gifts. Yet, rather than helping him celebrate his gifts, his employer increasingly assigns him projects far outside his interests and competencies. This creates deep frustration and confusion.

Ron, on the other hand, hasn't held a position that fits his gifting for several years. After spending twelve satisfying years with the same company, he has held four different positions in the last six years. He earns less today than he did ten years ago. Understandably, his self-worth and dignity are at a low point. He feels like a failure.

These men are not alone. Many men today are groping for a deeper sense of worth and contribution. They long for a calling that can satisfy their deep desire for value and meaning.

Besides the obvious differences in anatomy, a man has different instincts than a woman. By nature men are drawn to gather, hunt, explore, adventure, and conquer—we want to give ourselves to a mission. Why do young men dream about becoming explorers, discoverers, adventurers, warriors, and knights? It is because we each have been created by God to spend ourselves in a worthy cause.

A man even told me once, "Under certain circumstances I would be willing to die for you." Where does that come from? There is a noble impulse to manhood inside each of us.

Men are made for the task. It is our starting place, our most innate need, and the underlying motivator of our behavior. A man on an important mission is a happy man. It is what brings us joy, pleasure, peace, and contentment. How many times have you said, felt, heard a man say, or said to yourself:

- "I want my life to count—to make a difference!"
- "I need to feel like my life is going somewhere—that I have a direction."
- "I believe that I was created for a purpose."
- "I want to do something worthwhile with my life."
- "I want my life to matter. I need a mission. I need a cause into which I can invest myself."
- "I want to invest in the lives of people around me."
- "I want it to mean something that I have walked the face of the planet."
- "I don't want to be a shooting star that streaks across the sky one night—then disappears."

This compelling desire animates not just great explorers, missionaries, and top managers but all men. And not just the "great" men. Michael Novak, in *Business as a Calling*, says,

> Being a middle manager is not primarily a way station on the way to the top.... Middle management, many know early, is their calling. They want to be super good at it. They want to make a contribution. Most of all, they need to know in their own minds that they have done so.[1]

Whether he is a middle manager or a heating and cooling technician, every man has an inbred, intuitive sense that he is created to make a difference. As men, we are not frustrated because we think significance cannot be found. Rather, we are sure it can be found, and our frustration is that we have not yet taken hold of it.

Viktor Frankl, survivor of four Nazi concentration camps, tells the story of a diplomat who began psychiatric therapy because he was unhappy in his work. The psychiatrist repeatedly urged the diplomat to reconcile his relationship with his father. Yet after five years he was more unhappy than ever. He went to see Frankl.

After a few meetings, it was clear that this man's desire for meaning was frustrated by his vocation. He yearned to engage in some other line of work. At

Frankl's urging he changed jobs and became quite content.[2]

Frankl's point: In most cases of unhappiness we need only assist a man (or woman) to find meaning in his life. As Frankl says, "Man's search for meaning is the primary motivation in his life."[3]

A man will feel most alive, most useful, and most significant when he is doing what he was created to do. How happy would a lion be if he couldn't roar? How happy would an eagle be if he couldn't fly? How happy would a porpoise be if he couldn't swim?

WHAT YOU CAN DO | *Help Men Find Their Cause*

Pastors, this is a lay-up. If we simply and concretely show men how they can find purpose and meaning in the gospel, most will respond. Men love a challenge. Use these ideas to incite your men:

- Tell them, "Until you find a cause worth dying for, you will not have a cause worth living for."

- Tell them, "I would rather die for a worthy cause than live for no reason."

- Quote President Woodrow Wilson, who said, "I would rather fail in a cause that will ultimately succeed than succeed in a cause that will ultimately fail."

- Quote Dwight L. Moody, who one day heard, "The world has yet to see what God will do with, and for, and through, and in, and by the man who is fully and wholly consecrated to him." Moody thought, "He said a man. He did not say a great man, nor a learned man, nor a rich man, nor a wise man, nor an eloquent man, nor a smart man, but simply 'a man.' I am a man, and it lies with the man himself whether he will, or will not, make that entire and full consecration. I will try my utmost to be that man."[4]

- You don't have to say it will be easy. Writer Bruce Barton noted that Jesus called forth men's greatest efforts not by a promise of great rewards, but great obstacles.

A man doing what he was created to do will be a happy man. The apostle Paul tells us that we were created in Christ to do good works (Ephesians 2:10). Jesus says, "This is to my father's glory, that you bear much fruit" (John 15:8).

2. A *COMPANION*—SOMEONE TO SHARE LIFE WITH

Second, men want *someone* to share this with. This is the need for relationships, love, family, community, and acceptance.

Most men mainly look for this in a woman with whom they can share their lives. "The Lord God said, 'It is not good for the man to be alone. I will make a helper suitable for him'" (Genesis 2:18). Marriage is the mysterious, mystical fusion of two separate lives headed in two separate directions into what the Bible intriguingly calls "one flesh." Marriage is the highest order of human relationship, and there isn't a close second. Even children phase in and out of our lives.

It's no secret that men are more task-oriented and women are more relationship-oriented. Anyone who ever attended a Labor Day picnic knows this. The men huddle up to exaggerate about football and cars, while the women gather to swap stories about their children.

I realize these are stereotypes, but stereotypes work because they are generally true. For example, in the following pairings, which would you most likely assign to a man and which to a woman?

- Head and heart
- Logic and feeling
- Task and relationship
- Provider and nurturer

You no doubt picked *head, logic, task,* and *provider* as the "man" words. Even so, men are also relationship-oriented. And some men thrive on relationships. Even the most hardened taskmaster will be a lonely fool if he has nobody with whom to share his joys and sorrows.

That's why in the great movies, the hero always repairs to his love interest so she can share in his victory or console his defeat. A man goes out and hunts his bear, but then brings it home to get approval from his wife. Oswald Chambers put it like this: "The last sign of intimacy is to share secret joys."

On a scuba diving trip with my son and friends, we all felt that our grouchy divemaster was at the least disinterested in us and probably despised us for reasons unknown. Later, I struck up a conversation with him. He told me that three days earlier the woman he lived with for six years had found out he was cheating on her and thrown him out. They had essentially lived as a married couple, and this was tantamount to a divorce. At six feet two with bulging biceps he looked mean as a snake, yet he was reduced to putty over the woman he had betrayed.

We talked about the pain of hurting someone we love. Then he said, "Basically, I'm an [expletive for a centrally located bodily orifice]." He was in as much pain as any man I can remember. He had lost his "someone." However, since he had no faith foundation, he was stymied about what to do next.

Then he said something that is enough to drive a man to Christ. He said, "My life doesn't make any sense right now." By losing his "someone to share it with," he had lost part of his reason for living. We talked about grace, forgiveness, and God.

WHAT YOU CAN DO | *Help Men Value a Companion*

• Tell your men: The party will be over soon. There will only be two rocking chairs sitting side by side. Doesn't it make sense to invest today in the woman who will be sitting next to you then?

• Teach your men: No amount of success at work will ever be adequate to compensate for failure at home.

• Disciple your men to prove their love by the way they spend their time. Relationships create responsibilities, and the chief responsibility of relationships is time. Challenge your men to give time to whom time is due.

---

3. A *CONVICTION*—A SYSTEM THAT EXPLAINS WHY LIFE IS SO DIFFICULT

Third, men want a *conviction*—a belief in a system that gives a reasonable explanation for why numbers 1 and 2 are so difficult.

A man visited our Bible study and told me, "I have achieved everything I wanted—a luxury home, a beautiful wife, perfect kids, a high-powered job, and lots of money. Not long ago I deposited a $100,000 check into my account. That evening, my wife and I had a drink to celebrate, but I was downcast. She said, 'What do you want?' I had to tell her, 'I don't know.'"

Another man seemed to have it all together: professing Christian, great career, and a lovely wife who was three months pregnant. He chucked the whole thing and left her.

Even if we have a crystal-clear calling and the world's most perfect mate, it's hard. We must do our work while feeling the prick of thorns. This raises questions like the following:

- Why is life so hard?
- Will my life make a difference?
- How can I find peace in my relationships?
- If there is a God, does He know what I'm going through? (the issue of His omniscience)
- If He knows, does He care? (the issue of His omni-benevolence)
- If He cares, can He do anything about it? (the issue of His omnipotence)
- What happens when I die?

These are the kinds of questions addressed by all belief systems, philosophies, worldviews, and religions. Christianity and secularism are not trying to solve different problems. They are trying to solve the same problems in different ways.

Christianity is a system (a belief system) that perfectly explains why life is so hard, and what to do about it. The problem, however, is that every other system (philosophy, worldview, religion) also promises the same thing. And the good ones actually work—sometimes for as long as forty years. But all systems other than Christianity eventually fail, frequently at the worst possible moment, and often after your men have given that system the best years of their lives. So men at that point are not only hurting, but skeptical and suspicious.

All belief systems other than Christianity are counterfeits. All systems other than Christianity rest on foundations that are not true. Then how do these false systems remain in existence? That's because all systems have traces of truth—or they would never make it into circulation in the first place. As a philosophy professor of mine is fond of saying, "It takes a lot of truth to float an error."

Christianity is the only system that is all true all the time. Fortunately, the Bible doesn't describe a utopian world free of pain. That would make Christianity a wishful farce. Instead, the Bible describes the world exactly as we see it—a fallen world, but not without what Francis Schaeffer called "leftover beauty." The Bible describes a world groaning in pain that needs a Redeemer, Sanctifier, and Sustainer.

More importantly, the Bible describes how a man can rise above futility, sin, and despair and find peace, hope, and victory by surrendering his life to the lordship of Jesus Christ. The irony of surrender is that it leads not to defeat but victory.

WHAT YOU CAN DO | *Help Men Embrace Their Christian Conviction*

- Exhort your men not to give the best years of their lives to a lie. And accept that advice yourself by living a surrendered life.

- The irony of surrender is that it leads not to defeat but victory.

SO WHAT DO THESE THREE WANTS LOOK LIKE FROM DAY TO DAY?

Every man seeks the same ultimate thing. He may call it by many names: *happiness, success, contentment, fulfillment, pleasure, delight, love, peace, significance, purpose,* or *meaning.* Those words are all "placeholders" to describe a single overarching concept. He wants to experience joy in his life.

The question is: How does this pleasure, this fulfillment, this joy come to a man? What does he measure? How does he keep score? For most men, I believe this list of priorities captures most of what men want day to day:

1. To have a successful and satisfying *career*
2. To make enough *money* to be financially independent
3. To own a beautiful *home*
4. To have a good *wife*
5. To raise a happy *family*
6. To have an absorbing *sport* or *hobby*
7. To have good *health*

So he arrives home and asks her, "How was your day?"

She responds, "Good. How was your day?"

If today's progress equaled or exceeded what he wanted from these priorities, he answers, "Good."

Is it sinful to want career success, more money, to live in a nicer home, to drive a nice car, have a diversion you love, or to be able to take a nice vacation?

No, of course not—at least not necessarily—and these are good things to have. I know that I want them! But they are "second things." Unless a man is discipled to want what he *needs* (as discussed in chapter 5), he will settle for lesser things—mere *wants*, futilities that God has ordained to disappoint. As C. S.

Lewis put it, "You can't get second things by putting them first; you can get second things only by putting first things first."[5]

When he finally gets sick of answering, "Not so good"—that's when he will "want" to reexamine his conviction. That's when he will be interested in what he needs.

HOW TO GET READY FOR THE MEN WHO WILL BE COMING TO CHURCH NEXT SUNDAY

Let's say a man has driven past your church twice a day, to and from work, for ten years. What if he shows up with his family in tow next Sunday? It will make all the difference in the world if you and a team of leaders have thoroughly and repeatedly discussed questions like, "Why would he do that? Why would a man come through our front door? What is the problem he is trying to solve?"

Of course, there are many reasons (e.g., moral and religious instruction for children, spiritual vacuum, desire to find God). But whatever his reasons, it is good that he wants to come!

One thing we can be pretty sure about: when a man comes to church, he wants to find rest for his soul. Running after career success, managing a marriage, keeping up with kids, and making the mortgage payments is going to leave most men exhausted. We've created a culture that requires more energy than men have to give. Personally, if I were pastoring a church, I would hoist a sign over the entrance to our sanctuary that said:

To all who are weary and burdened, come and find rest.

I would keep the sanctuary a sanctuary.

Unfortunately, because there is so much to do, a lot of our churches emit the impression to men that Jesus said, "Come to me, all you who are weary and burdened, and I will give you more work to do."

Of course, what Jesus actually said was, "Come to me, all you who are weary and burdened, and I will give you rest. Take my yoke upon you and learn from me, for I am gentle and humble in heart, and you will find rest for your souls" (Matthew 11:28–29).

Work is part of discipleship—"This is to my Father's glory, that you bear much fruit, *showing yourselves to be my disciples*" (John 15:8 emphasis added)— but it is the last part. Is it right to ask a man to give away the little bit of Jesus he has when he doesn't yet have enough for himself? How tragic to have a man succeed in the work of the church but fail in his family. Let's be careful not to "send" men to work before we have "equipped" them to be godly men, husbands, and fathers. First, help men fill up in their relationships with Jesus. Once full, they will feel compelled by gratitude to serve.

They'll be coming in droves next Sunday. Let's get ready for them. Let's create a place for them to lay down their burdens. Let's not give men the impression that Christianity is merely exchanging one performance-based culture for another.

THE PASTOR'S TASK

In the movie *Black Hawk Down* a soldier said to his superior, "You really believe in this mission down to your very bones, don't you, Sergeant?"

The sergeant replied, "These people have no jobs, no food, no education, no future. I figure we have two things we can do: We can help, or we can sit back and watch the country destroy itself on CNN. I was trained to fight, how about you? I was trained to make a difference."

Training is a big deal. Twenty-five percent of Secret Service duty is training—their credo: "Repetitive training to overcome the negatives of self-sacrifice." For lack of training, a lot of men have not been able to make a difference—and they have settled for second things.

You are the key to training (discipling) your men.

WHAT YOU CAN DO | *Help Men Become Disciples*

• Train/disciple your men to understand how what they want fits into the larger picture of what God is doing in the world. Tell them: it is true that the Christian life is a broad road of happiness, joy, peace, blessing, success, significance, and contentment. Ironically, however, it is gained by choosing the narrow road of surrender, obedience, self-denial, self-sacrifice, truth, worship, and service.

• Give men what they need in the context of what they want. Knowing what men want is a key component of the pastoring-men skill set. In the next chapter, let's explore what keeps men from getting what they want.

Photocopy this chapter and discuss it with your leadership team.

POINTS TO REMEMBER

- All men want to be happy. They find happiness by finding three things:
  1. A *cause* we can give our lives to that will make a difference—a mission, significance, meaning, purpose
  2. A *companion* to share it with—relationships, love, family, acceptance
  3. A *conviction* that gives a reasonable explanation for why numbers 1 and 2 are so difficult—a belief system, worldview, philosophy, religion
- On a day-to-day basis, these are the priorities for most men:
  1. To have a successful and satisfying *career*
  2. To make enough *money* to be financially independent
  3. To own a beautiful *home*
  4. To have a good *wife*
  5. To raise a happy *family*
  6. To have an absorbing *sport* or *hobby*
  7. To have good *health*
- When men come to church, we need to give them what they need, but in the context of what they want.

WHAT KEEPS MEN FROM GETTING WHAT THEY WANT?

No man fails on purpose. Yet many men find it difficult to be a husband and father, find job contentment, keep themselves morally straight, and lead balanced lives. This chapter will give you a greater understanding of the challenges and opportunities that keep your men from getting what they want—their cause, companion, and conviction.

So what keeps men from getting what they want?

LIES: OUR NATIVE TONGUE

It begins with a lie—many lies, actually. There are two languages in the world: *truth* and *lies*. The first language—the native tongue of every man—is the language of lies. When the father of lies ruled our lives, "lies" was the only language we knew (John 8:43–44). Before I became a Christian, I would often lie even if the truth could have served me better. It was my native tongue—a language that flowed freely from my lower nature.

When you and I received Christ, we became bilingual. We learned a second language—the language of truth.

But what happens to anyone who doesn't regularly practice speaking their second language? They revert to their native tongue.

If we do not abide in Christ day by day, if we do not regularly practice our second language, we will revert to our native tongue. You know this is true because you know self-deceived Christians who regularly lie to you—and not about little things.

How do men fall back into their native language? Every morning your men go into a world where all day long they are tempted to exchange the truth of God for a lie (Romans 1:25).

All men either live by the truth or a good lie. This is another way of discussing the belief systems mentioned in the last chapter.

No individual, Christian or otherwise, will choose to live by an obvious lie. Which counterfeit dollar bill is most likely to make it into circulation? Isn't it the one that looks the most like the real thing? In the same way, the only lies that make it into circulation are ones that appear to be true. A good lie is probably only one or two degrees off course. Otherwise it would be rejected. The popular prosperity gospel is one example.

What does a good lie look like? A good lie can take many forms. For example, good lies about happiness might tell a man that to be happy he needs to . . .

- Make this much money
- Get that promotion
- Drive a certain car
- Have an hour a day for himself
- Achieve a certain desire or goal
- Lust after that woman
- Have his wife act differently
- Have his children behave better
- Have investments do well
- Be able to eat what he wants
- Have a ministry that gives him strokes

THE BIG LIE

Do men really "need" these things to be happy? Each of these statements boils down to this core lie: "Jesus is not enough to make me happy." Using all the media at his disposal—thousands of cell towers, TV antennae and satellites, newspapers, and even friends—the great deceiver Satan wants men to believe that God isn't capable of giving men true joy and contentment. This is the Big Lie.

As a pastor, it's good to remember that for every truth you tell your men, they are hearing hundreds of lies—many of them good lies—throughout the week.

WHAT YOU CAN DO | *About the Big Lie*

- Explain to your men that there are two languages in the world: truth and lies.

- Explain that all men either live by the truth or a good lie.

- Explain that it's not that easy to discern the difference between the truth and a really good lie.

- Expose or correct the prevailing "good" lies that sound very close to the truth.

- Some of your men are living by a good lie. They need to see how they have believed a false gospel.

- Some of your men are monolingual. They still only speak one language—lies. Regularly present those men with the gospel of truth.

- Some of your bilingual men have reverted to their native tongue. They need to be challenged.

- For your solid Christian men, remind them how we all must renew ourselves daily and abide in the truth of the gospel of our Lord and Savior Jesus Christ through faith and repentance.

- Explain to your men that a "good" lie will work—for as many as forty years. But a lie is still a lie, and eventually it will betray them, and usually at the worst possible moment.

IDOLS AND THE BIG LIE

Idols also keep men from getting what they want. I used to race a vintage Porsche and used racing as a platform to build relationships with men and share my faith. One day a man who never missed a chance to race asked me quite seriously, "When does my passion for racing become an idol?" Good question.

All idolatry is rooted in *unbelief.* This unbelief can take many forms, but at its root is the powerful lie, "Jesus Christ alone is not enough to make me happy. I need something else." An idol is something we worship. The issue is making anything besides the Trinity the object of our worship. It is looking to anything except Jesus Christ for identity, meaning, and ultimate purpose. An idol is anything that becomes an object of inordinate affection. An idol is anything of which we say, "I *must* have this to be happy."

John Calvin said that men are "idol factories." Perhaps nothing interferes with a man's faith more than the root problem of making idols—it's the "next step" after believing the Big Lie. The average American Christian male has made an idol of something that competes with his full surrender to the lordship of Christ. Men can make idols of almost anything, but common examples today include these:

- Money
- Titles and positions (especially if the job doesn't generate a large income)
- Homes (i.e., attaching personal worth and identity to a dwelling)
- Country club memberships (i.e., being part of the "right" crowd)
- Ministry titles (e.g., elder, deacon)
- Relationships (e.g., idolizing a wife)
- Affiliations with important people
- Cars, boats, planes, motorcycles
- Their bodies (i.e., physical appearance)
- Superior intelligence
- Their own righteousness
- The praise of men (what C.S. Lewis called "to win worship"[1])

As you can readily see, all these affections are horizontal, focused on people, things, and ourselves. All such friendship with the world is spiritual adultery (James 4:4).

Idols make promises they cannot keep, which is why you can be on a winning streak and still feel empty.

WHAT YOU CAN DO | *About Idols*

- Most men don't really understand the definition of an idol. Periodically define "idols" and give appropriate examples.

- Remind your men that we are "idol factories."

- Challenge your men to consider how they can make even their own spirituality into an idol—like a church position or exceptionally righteous behavior.

SUCCESS SICKNESS

Biblically speaking, three things keep men from getting what they want: the world, the flesh, and the devil. In practice, lies and idols infect many men with a disease we will call "success sickness."

Trent (not his real name) rose rapidly to become the youngest K-Mart manager in the history of the company. They sent him to troubleshoot a store that was losing $1,000,000 per year.

Trent supervised the renovation of the store, then orchestrated a turnaround from losing $1,000,000 a year to making $1,000,000 a year. He said, "I was part of that. When it was all over, I would get to work at the usual time, about 6:00 a.m., sit in the parking lot, look at the store all lit up, and ask myself, 'Why am I so miserable?'"

To not get what you want can be painful. Perhaps more painful, though, as Trent discovered, is to get what you want and still not be happy. Of course, a lot of men don't reach their goals. Many more men, however, do achieve their goals only to find out that success—at least success the way they had defined it—doesn't satisfy. What's that all about?

All men want to be successful in what they do. That's normal and healthy. However, many men get carried away with their idols and end up contracting a bad case of "success sickness."

Success sickness is the disease of always wanting more, but never being happy when you get it. We are the nation that weeps if we only win a silver medal. Success sickness is the intangible pain of not achieving goals that should have never been set or, like Trent, achieving them only to find they didn't really matter.

The greatest problem we see in our work at Man in the Mirror is not that men are failing to achieve their goals. In most cases, they are achieving them. The problem is, they are the wrong goals. Many men get what they want only to find it doesn't matter. We all know that failure means to not get what you want. However, we could also say failure means to succeed in a way that doesn't really matter.

The unhappy result of believing the "success will make you happy" lie is that many men today are struggling with problems that success can't solve. As Michael Novak pointed out, "The aftertaste of affluence is boredom."[2]

Regrettably, many men don't learn this lesson until they've given it ten, twenty, or more years—often the best years of their lives. What a strategic opportunity to pastor men about success sickness and success that matters.

WHAT YOU CAN DO | *About Success Sickness*

• Explain how lies and idols lead to success sickness.

• Describe success sickness to your men.

• Challenge your men to consider to what extent they have this disease.

If applicable, be vulnerable about your own struggles in this and all other areas we're discussing.

Now let's discuss three symptoms of "success sickness."

SYMPTOMS OF SUCCESS SICKNESS

The Rat Race

The first symptom of success sickness is the rat race. Picture men, lots of men, men under pressure, zooming down the fast lanes of life, straining to keep pace. Some are oblivious to what they're doing. Some are starting to wonder about it. Others are weary. Still others have "hit the wall."

What is the rat race? The rat race is the conflict between who man is *created* to be and who he is *tempted* to be. It is the endless pursuit of an ever increasing prosperity that ends in frustration rather than contentment.

So how do men get caught up in the rat race? Galatians 5:7 asks the question this way: "You were running a good race. Who cut in on you to keep you from obeying the truth?" Paul teaches the answer two verses later: "A little yeast works through the whole batch of dough" (verse 9). That "yeast" is the man's lie of choice.

Francis Schaeffer, noted cultural commentator of the twentieth century, explained that most American adults have adopted two impoverished values: *personal peace*, not wanting to be bothered with the troubles of others, and *affluence*, a life made up of things, things, and more things.[3] A friend sheepishly told me that he has a weakness for golf clubs. He has ten expensive drivers in his closet. Ironically, it's the old beat-up one that's his favorite.

In our work with men we regularly meet men who have "prayed a prayer" for salvation, but for the last five, ten, fifteen, or more years they have been living by their own ideas. They have built on the foundation of their own best thinking. They read the Bible for comfort, but the *Wall Street Journal* for direction.

They seek personal prosperity, often at the expense of family.

The result is that many men have been knocked off balance. Pursuing their career goals, they neglect their wives emotionally, and slowly, the two of them grow apart. Taking a cue from dad, their kids often run in their own mini-rat races, and dads sometimes feel left out and unappreciated. Twenty years later it slowly dawns on these men that they gave their best years to careers that promised what they couldn't deliver. In fact, a man will often feel "dumped on" and "used" in his career, a festering bitterness that only further infects the other areas of his life.

The rat race charges an expensive toll. It will take everything men have to give.

Eventually, they begin to ask the painful questions: "What's it all about? How can I be so successful and so unfulfilled at the same time? Is this all there is? There must be more. There's gotta be."

Who are these men? They are your men. They are the men who visit your church. And they are the men who drive by your church several times a week on their way to and from work, wondering if you have answers, but not yet able to muster the courage to walk through your front door.

WHAT YOU CAN DO | *About Men Running in the Rat Race*

- From time to time, draw men's attention to the difference between the rat race and God's race.

Invite men to discuss how the rat race is affecting them, and what your church can do to help men—both the men you already have and the men you would like to have.

The Unexamined Life

The second symptom of success sickness is leading an unexamined life. Evan was the national sales manager for his company. One day he traveled to Texas to spend a day making calls with one of his salesmen. At the end of the day that salesman, Steve, walked Evan into the airport to catch his plane back to the Midwest.

As they parted, Steve said, "Evan, you're amazing the way you sell our product. You're brilliant. But as smart as you are, you baffle me. You don't have a clue about where you came from, you don't have a clue about where you're going, and you don't have a clue about your purpose in life."

With that, Steve turned and walked away. For months and months Evan kept hearing Steve's searing comments over and over.

Many people had prayed for Evan's spiritual salvation over the years. In February of the following year, Evan was invited to an evangelistic event where he gave his life to Jesus Christ. In April he had a heart attack at the age of forty-four, and faced bypass surgery.

The night before the surgery, he took his wife out to dinner. Evan told her how he had an incredible peace and calm. His wife, Tracie, on the other hand, was a basket case. Tracie held a PhD in education and worked at the local university.

Evan took her hand and said words that echoed those he had heard a year earlier. "Tracie, you're amazing when it comes to education. You're brilliant. But as smart as you are, you baffle me. You don't have a clue about where you came from, you don't have a clue about where you're going, and you don't have a clue about your purpose in life."

Tracie stared out the window.

Evan had learned from Steve and others. He realized that men face no greater temptation than the tendency to lead unexamined lives. He had learned that to lead an unexamined life means to rush from task to busy task without taking time-outs to reflect on life's larger meaning and purpose.

Such a pace robs men—and women too—of purpose.

I love technology. Technology is a friend, but this friend also has a dark side. As a man increases his labor-saving devices, he also increases his workload and the access other people have to him. The drone of these devices often leaves a man with no place to sit and simply think.

Socrates said, "Know thyself," and Plato wrote, "The unexamined life is not worth living." When men choose to run the gauntlet of the rat race, they barter away their times of reflection and self-examination.

Most men have not carefully chiseled their worldview by a personal search for truth and obedience to God and his Word. Rather, they are drifting. They are not thinking deeply about their lives. Buffeted by the whipping winds of daily pressure and tossed about by surging waves of change, men long for the sure-footed sands of simpler days. They have scarcely a clue of how to reach such a place.

Lamentations 3:40 exhorts, "Let us examine our ways and test them, and let us return to the Lord." Only on the anvil of self-examination can God shape a man into the image of His Son. "Teach us to number our days, that we may gain a heart of wisdom" (Psalm 90:12).

Pastoring men is all about holding up a mirror in front of men so they can examine their lives. When men come to your church, showing them their reflections in a mirror is something they have implicitly given you permission to do.

WHAT YOU CAN DO | *About the Unexamined Life*

• Lead your men into self-examination through your sermons.

• Teach your men to periodically call "time-outs" for personal reflection and self-examination.

The Cultural Christian

We are discussing how success sickness keeps men from getting what they want. The third symptom of success sickness is cultural Christianity. Many men who are seeking material success have become cultural Christians. Years ago, as a businessman who wanted to be a disciple, I vacillated between two sets of heroes. On one hand, I was inspired by great businessmen who lived for God—the likes of Walt Meloon, who built Correct Craft into the world's premier brand of ski and wakeboarding boats.[4] I also wanted to emulate heroes of the faith like C. S. Lewis, Jim Dobson, Tom Skinner, and Bill Bright. On the other hand, I secretly aspired to the accomplishments and fortunes of business barons like Trammel Crow, Warren Buffet, Bill Gates, and Malcolm Forbes. I was torn between becoming a disciple of Wall Street or Church Street.

When I hit the ten-year mark in my spiritual journey, I realized something was desperately wrong with my life, but I couldn't put my finger on any one problem. I was an active Christian, reading my Bible and praying regularly, immersed in church life, a vocal witness, and pursuing a moral lifestyle.

Curiously, I was sitting at the top of my career. Materially, I was taken care of wonderfully. Yet, when I would imagine another man thinking how I was blessed, I would want to grab him by the arms, shake him, and scream, "You don't understand! This isn't a blessing; it's a curse!"

Finally the intangible pain became so strong that I called a "time-out" for reflection and self-examination—which I thought would last a couple of weeks.

I spent the next two and a half years staring at my navel.

At first all I could grasp were some of the thoughts described in chapter 2, "How Are Your Men Doing?"

- I was tired.
- I had a lingering feeling something wasn't quite right about my life.
- My life wasn't turning out the way I had planned.
- I felt like my life was coming unglued.
- I didn't feel like anyone really cared about me, personally.
- I was achieving my goals, but success didn't satisfy.

A couple of years later during a major business crisis, a thought went through my mind as I was sitting in the rubble of my collapsing empire: *There is a God we want and there is a God who is. They are not the same God. The turning point of our lives is when we stop seeking the God we want and start seeking the God who is.*

I realized I had become what we might call a *cultural* Christian. In *The Man in the Mirror* I defined the term *cultural Christianity*—the mindset of every cultural Christian—this way:

Cultural Christianity means to seek the God we want instead of the God who is. It is the tendency to be shallow in our understanding of God, wanting Him to be more of a gentle grandfather type who spoils us and lets us have our own way. It is sensing a need for God, but on our own terms. It is wanting the God we have underlined in our Bibles without wanting the rest of Him, too. It is God relative instead of God absolute.[5]

When is a man a cultural Christian? Men become cultural Christians when they seek the God (or gods) they want, and not the God who is.

Men who are cultural Christians read their Bibles with an agenda, if they read them at all. They decide in advance what they want, and then read their Bibles looking for evidence to support the decisions they have already made. In short, they follow the God they are underlining in their Bibles, which is like making a "fifth" gospel.

In many ways they have merely added Jesus to their lives as another interest in an already crowded schedule. They practice a kind of "Spare Tire Christianity." They keep Jesus in the trunk just in case they have a flat.

They have made a plan for their lives. Their credo is, "Plan, then pray." Their lives are shaped more by following the herds of commerce than the footsteps of Christ.

Biblically, these men have let the worries of this life and the deceitfulness of money choke the word and make it unfruitful (Matthew 13:22), have let the yeast of culture work through the whole batch of dough (Galatians 5:9), and are high risk for a great crash because they built on sand and not on the rock (Matthew 7:24–27).

They want to have their cake and eat it, too. The technical term for this is *syncretism*, "the blending or attempt to combine differing philosophical or religious beliefs."

"Success sickness" is based upon a lie, and it is killing us. No wonder so many men feel what Søren Kierkegaard called "the sickness unto death."

I once read of a survey from the Billy Graham Evangelistic Association that 90 percent of all Christians lead defeated lives. "Defeated" is a great way to describe a man who has one or more of these three success sickness symptoms—the rat race, the unexamined life, or living as a cultural Christian. If we are not careful, it can be a terminal illness.

WHAT YOU CAN DO | *About Cultural Christians*

- Teach your men the difference between a cultural Christian and a biblical Christian. Use Matthew 13:22 to describe the cultural Christian and Matthew 13:23 to describe the biblical Christian.

HOW GOD DEALS WITH MEN WHO MAKE IDOLS

Earlier I said that, biblically speaking, three things—three temptations—keep men from getting what they want: the world, the flesh, and the devil. That is completely true, but it is also true that God Himself keeps men from being satisfied with what they get from their vain pursuits. When men pursue idols, He will not let that stand. Here's the equation:

Men make idols + God hates idols = We've got a problem

God will not force us to revere Him, but He will make it impossible for us to be happy unless we do.

Here are three ways God will "deal" with us as men when we make an idol:

1. *He will withhold the thing we think we can't live without.* I spent the first fifteen years of my adult life working and praying to achieve something that would have destroyed me, then was disappointed when I was spared. It is a mercy to not receive that which will destroy you. "When you ask, you do not receive, because you ask with wrong motives, that you may spend what you get on your pleasures" (James 4:3).

2. *He will remove the thing we think we can't live without.* There is another name besides "idol" for something we think we can't live without—*addiction.* The problem with addictions is that we can't stop on our own. That's why God has to "help" us. Contractions, whether business or personal, often reflect God's loving discipline. He removes the shakable kingdom so the unshakable kingdom may remain: "The words 'once more' indicate the removing of what can be shaken—that is, created things—so that what cannot be shaken may remain" (Hebrews 12:27).

3. *He will give us so much of the thing we want that we gag on it.* Think of the Israelites who got tired of manna and asked for meat. God said, "Meat? You want meat? I'll give you meat." Numbers 11:19 (NLT) says, "You will eat it for a whole month until you gag and are sick of it. For you have rejected the Lord." Sometimes God wins our complete allegiance by showing us the emptiness of any other allegiance.

Nevertheless, God still tends to under-discipline, not over-discipline. "The Lord is compassionate and gracious, slow to anger, abounding in love. He will not always accuse, nor will he harbor his anger forever; *he does not treat us as our sins deserve* or repay us according to our iniquities" (Psalm 103:8–10, emphasis added).

WHAT YOU CAN DO | *With Men Who Make Idols*

- Think of a few of your men who are struggling. How can this model help you understand what God may be doing in their lives?

- How can this taxonomy help you pastor your men more effectively?

- Teach all your men the three ways God deals with us when we make idols.

IT'S ABOUT SURRENDER

Once a man told "Jack," a friend of mine, "I could never become a Christian because I could never give up beer and cigarettes."

"Oh, I drink all the beer and smoke all the cigarettes I want," Jack quickly replied.

"You do?" the man asked. That eventually led to a meaningful presentation of the gospel. Actually, Jack didn't drink any beer or smoke any cigarettes. Jack told the guy that, although he could have all he wanted, he didn't want any. That's because Jack had lost his taste for them. God had changed the desires of his heart.

A man will never fully get what he wants until he fully surrenders to the lordship of Christ. Ironically, when he does surrender, God changes the desires of his heart to want what God wants.

POINTS TO REMEMBER

- There are two languages in the world: truth and lies.
- All men either live by the truth or a good lie.
- A "good" lie will work—for as many as forty years. But a lie is still a lie, and eventually it will betray a man, and usually at the worst possible moment.
- Men are "idol factories."
- All idolatry is rooted in *unbelief.*
- Success sickness is the disease of always wanting more, but never being happy when you get it.
- Failure means to succeed in a way that doesn't matter.
- Three symptoms of success sickness are that men (1) get caught up in the rat race; (2) lead unexamined lives; and (3) become cultural rather than biblical Christians.
- God deals three ways with men who make idols: (1) He *withholds* something the man thinks he cannot live without; (2) He *removes* something the man thinks he cannot live without; or (3) He *gives* the man so much of what he wants that he "gags" on it.
- A man will never fully get what he wants until he fully surrenders to the lordship of Christ.

REACH YOUR MEN

WHAT DO MEN NEED, AND HOW CAN YOU GIVE IT TO THEM?

Once upon a time there was a manufacturing plant that produced an equal number of trousers and dresses. The plant prospered—three shifts ran around the clock. Nearly everyone in town worked there and, of course, wore trousers and dresses.

THE PARABLE CONTINUES . . .

It remained that way for generations. But about fifty years later, when some of the grandchildren had grown up, they became bored with factory work, especially the ones who wore trousers. They felt most of the trousers—and many of the dresses—manufactured at the plant were out of style. *These clothes just aren't relevant to the times*, they thought. So they left to search for a better life.

With fewer people in town, the demand for trousers and dresses began to decline, especially for trousers; in fact the plant was producing only half as many trousers as dresses.

Few noticed the change day to day, but after a couple of decades the plant—which had the capacity to run three shifts—was down to a single shift. That left a tremendous unused productive capacity, though hardly anyone seemed to notice and even fewer made a fuss. After all, the troublemakers had left, and those who remained seemed content to leave well enough alone.

Because the demand they did have was heavily weighted toward dresses, plant management, as you might expect, increasingly catered to the dress division. When management felt they could afford to purchase new equipment, they naturally bought it for the dress division, since that's where the sales were.

Dress purchasers insisted the plant keep up with current styles, but management rarely heard from trousers at all. So the dress division received a large budget for new product design, while trousers hardly received any budget at all.

Since more people worked in dresses than trousers, most of management's time focused on dresses. Each year they spent less time thinking about trousers, and trousers became terribly out of step with the times. In fact, some of the designs had not changed in decades. The trousers they did make seemed to be of inferior quality—not able to stand up to normal wear and tear, nor the demands of everyday life. Since the plant wasn't making as many trousers, there just weren't enough good ones to go around.

It became a vicious downward spiral. In fact, conditions deteriorated so far that poor trousers sales eventually threatened to bring down dresses too.

Some of the more perceptive people began to ask, "Why can't they make trousers the way they used to?" Eventually, a few of the more innovative plant managers began to explore ways to solve the problem.

Management realized that if they were ever going to get the factory back to full capacity, they would need some fresh ideas to increase trouser production. They would have to design some new products to attract purchasers, stimulate demand for new trousers, retrain some managers, and retool the assembly lines to make quality trousers.

They knew they would need to find raw materials that could be made into trousers, get them into the plant, and start producing trousers suited for the times. The managers were excited and dreamed about adding a second shift. But they weren't quite sure where to start.

SOLVING THE RIGHT PROBLEM

In this chapter we will answer the all-important question, "What do men need?" Like the plant managers in the parable, where do you start?

It is easy to look at the data and come to the wrong conclusion. When you and

I are at work, all day long we look at "the data." If we rely on our own best thinking, we will often come to the wrong conclusion. We will believe those we should not, disbelieve those we should, pick the wrong people for leadership, launch the wrong programs, and fear our friends while embracing those who oppose us. Consider just three historical examples.

The men of Israel made a treaty because the Gibeonites showed them moldy bread, cracked wineskins, old clothes, and claimed to come from a distant country. This was a clever ruse—they lived nearby. Where did the men of Israel go wrong? Joshua 9:14 (NLT) says, "So the Israelites examined their food, but they did not consult the Lord." The men of Israel came to the wrong conclusion because they looked at the data, but didn't ask God for direction.

Frankly, our men also put on a ruse. They put on their "game faces" so we will think everything is "just perfect." And then, when they crack, it's tempting to give them a social worker's or a psychologist's answer.

For forty days the troops of Israel listened to Goliath and cowered in fear. David looked the giant over once and said, "Don't worry about a thing. I can take him. The battle is the Lord's." Armed with confidence in God, he then went out and killed Israel's enemy. It is easy to look at the data and come to the wrong conclusion, as the soldiers did. The "men problem" is a Goliath, but God has called pastors to "take him."

Samuel, sent to anoint one of Jesse's sons to be the next king, on seeing Eliab thought to himself, "Surely he is the one!" But the Lord said, "Don't judge by his appearance or height. . . . The Lord doesn't see things the way you see them. People judge by outward appearance, but the Lord looks at the heart" (1 Samuel 16:7 NLT). If you have been a pastor for very long, you know how easy it is to look at the data and come to the wrong conclusion. You have a growing list of failed initiatives that promised to grow your men but were not sustainable. You are tired of "clever." All along you knew in your heart, "There are no shortcuts."

THE BIBLICAL SOLUTION

We can give men what they really need if, instead of looking at the data, we ask God for direction. Fortunately, in the Bible, Jesus has already given the church its direction. In this chapter we will see that, despite the complexity of men's lives, there is a single, golden solution. Jesus called His followers "disciples." And Jesus told those of us who are already disciples to go and make more disciples—starting at home.

What men need is to become disciples of our Lord and Savior Jesus Christ, and all that this implies. It is a single concept that fully captures the essence of what it means to be "in Christ."

I know you will agree that people often use the same word to mean different things, or different words to mean the same thing. So before going further, let's make sure we mean the same thing when we say "disciple."

WHAT IS A DISCIPLE?

To be a disciple of Jesus is the highest honor to which a man can aspire. Yet even though discipleship is one of the hottest topics in Christendom today, it's also one of the least understood.

Perhaps when most people hear the terms "making disciples" or "discipleship" they visualize a curriculum. That would make a "disciple" *someone who knows a lot about their faith.* And that is partially true. To excel at anything you need to have the right information. But to be a disciple is a much deeper, richer, and fuller concept. It is also a lifelong process of becoming more like Jesus. It starts with salvation, matures through learning, and fulfills by loving and serving our neighbors.

What then is a *disciple?* We all know that the Greek word *mathetes* means a "learner" or "pupil." However, when applied to the early Christians, the term "disciple" came to mean someone who had declared a personal allegiance to the teachings and person of Jesus.

Here's a good working definition: A disciple is someone **called** to live "in" Christ, **equipped** to live "like" Christ, and **sent** to live "for" Christ. "Calling" includes professing faith and abiding in Christ (John 1:12, 8:31–32). "Equipping" includes the ongoing process of spiritual formation, growth, and maturity (2 Timothy 3:16–17, Colossians 1:28–29). "Sending" includes discipling others, doing good works, bearing much fruit, and neighbor love (Matthew 28:18–20, Ephesians 2:10, John 15:8, John 13:34–35).

The reason I like this definition is that it is both *biblical* and *actionable.* Because it uses terms found in the Bible, we don't have to quibble over the words. And because the meanings are concrete, you can use these three rubrics to recruit men to specific responses, such as praying to receive Jesus (calling), getting them in small groups (equipping), or serving on a committee or missions trip (sending).

Men tend to look for what's practical. They want and need a practical, not theoretical, understanding of what it means to be a disciple of Jesus, and how to live it out daily as regular guys.

Figure 1 lays out some of the biblical support for this definition:

TEXT	CALL	EQUIP	SEND
Matt 28:18-20	**Baptize** in name of Father, Son, Spirit	**Teach** to obey	**Go** and make disciples
Luke 6:47	**Comes** to me	**Hears** my words	Puts them into **practice**
2 Tim. 3:15-17	**Salvation** through faith in Christ Jesus	Teach, rebuke, correct, train to thoroughly **equip**	For every **good work**
Isa. 6:7-8	Guilt **taken away** and sin **atoned** for		Whom shall I **send**? Who will go for us?
Acts 26:20	**Repent** and **turn** to God		Prove repentance by **deeds**
Eph. 2:8-10	**Saved** by grace through faith		To do **good works**
Matt. 13:37-38	**Love God** with all heart, soul, mind		**Love neighbor** as yourself
John 3:3	Must be **born again**		
Matt. 7:24		**Hear** my words	Put into **practice**
2 Tim. 2:2		**Entrust teachings** to reliable people	Qualified to **teach others**
John 20:21			As the Father sent me, so I am sending you
John 13:34-35 (Rom. 13:7) (Luke 7:12)			All men know my disciples if you **love** one another
John 8:31			If you **hold to** my teaching, you are really my disciples
John 15:8			Bear much **fruit** showing self to be my disciples
Matt. 7:12			**Do to others** what you would want done to you. Sums up law and prophets.
Luke 14:27			Must **carry cross** and **follow Jesus** to be His disciple
Gen. 1:27-28 (Psalm 8:6-8)			Be fruitful, fill, subdue, and rule over **creation**

FIGURE 1

Biblical Support for the Definition of *Disciple* as One Called, Equipped, and Sent

As you can see from figure 1, the Bible makes a strong case that *calling, equipping, and sending are a sort of "trinity" for making disciples.* Men can get their minds around these three actionable components of discipleship—church staffs and leadership too! Isn't that what we all want? For the rest of the chapter, we will explore each in more detail.

CALLING MEN TO CHRIST

First and foremost, men need to become born again. A disciple is *called* to profess faith in Jesus Christ—*evangelism.* Jesus said, "I have come to call sinners" (Mark 2:17).

I grew up in what we thought was a "Christian home," but we didn't know Christ. We didn't reject the gospel; we never heard it. Our church was focused on other things. In my early twenties, though, my soon-to-be wife, Patsy, explained the gospel of Jesus to me, and I soon embraced Christ as my Lord and Savior.

There are about 120 million men in America fifteen years of age and older.[1] Regrettably, about 60 percent, or 70 million,[2] of these men have made no profession of faith in Christ. That's sad, because many of them would gladly receive Christ if engaged in a credible way. What's even sadder, though, is how many men think they have tried Christianity, found it wanting, and rejected it, when in fact they have never properly understood it.

There's no other way to say it. To be truly happy a man must be born again—to surrender his life to Jesus. To be born again is the right starting point. And unless a man has the right starting point, everything else will turn out wrong.

This may be more difficult for men who already believe they are Christians than for those who know they are not. Søren Kierkegaard wondered of his countrymen, "Are all who call themselves Christian, Christian?" Today, it just does not seem possible that all the men who claim to believe in Jesus have truly and earnestly repented of their sins and embraced Jesus by faith.

C. S. Lewis once said, "Before you can make a man a Christian you must first help him understand that he is a pagan." D. L. Moody put it like this: "You've got to get people lost before you can get them saved."

This is exactly what Jesus proceeded to do with the religious Nicodemus in John 3:3: "Very truly I tell you, no one can see the kingdom of God unless they are born again."

Jesus Christ has issued a divine summons to salvation. He has commanded men everywhere to repent (Acts 17:30). Once a man has professed faith, he should be baptized, as applicable, in accordance with your tradition.

Salvation should be made as simple as possible, but not oversimplified. I once heard a speaker say to eight hundred leaders in our community, "If you want to go to heaven and receive eternal life, all you have to do is pray this prayer." There was no mention of why men need a Savior. There was no mention of "sin" or "the cross." That was a gross misstatement of the gospel. Jesus did say to count the cost.

When Are Men "Callable"?

It makes sense to fish for men when they're "biting." Your ministry to "call" men to Christ will be most effective if you connect with them when they face a turning point or crisis. Here is my list of reachable moments. You will no doubt be able to add to this list:

Searching for a purpose	Searching for an identity	A lack of meaning
Loneliness	Emptiness	Marriage
Divorce	Out of wedlock pregnancy	Birth of a child
Loss of a child	First job	Fired from job
Business failure	Financial crisis	Moral failure
Midlife crisis	Stalled career	Failed romance
Loss of physical strength	Sense of mortality	Empty nest
Health crisis	Aging parents	Loss of parents

Find a man's point of pain and you'll find an open door. Be there for men when they feel a need. Appeal to what men want, not what they don't really care about. For example, attract a man to your church service or event by offering a topic with a title like "How to Find True Success." From there you can segue to "How Jesus Gives Us Abundant Life." The more we touch on their wants (their felt needs), the more sticky our ministries will be.

Commitment versus Surrender

Once Adrian Rogers, the famous Baptist preacher, went on a mission trip to Romania. Over the course of two weeks he bonded with his interpreter, but hadn't learned much about his thoughts. So toward the end of the trip he asked, "Tell me what you think of American Christians."

"I don't want to talk about it," came the strange reply. This, of course, only made Dr. Rogers more curious, so he began to press him for an answer.

After several attempts he finally said, "Why won't you tell me? I really want to know."

Finally, the interpreter capitulated. "Well, okay then, but you're not going to like my answer. I don't think you Americans understand what Christianity is all about. Back in the 1960s you began to use the word 'commitment' to describe your relationship with Christ.

"However, any time a word comes into usage, another word goes into disuse. Until the 1960s you Americans talked about surrender to Christ. Surrender means giving up control, turning over all to the Master Jesus.

"By changing to the word 'commitment' your relationship with Christ has become something you do; therefore you are able to keep control. Surrender means giving up all rights to one's self. You Americans don't like to do that so, instead, you make a commitment."[3]

It is worth pondering.

Men need to become disciples of Jesus, and the first thing this implies is that they must be born again.

WHAT YOU CAN DO | *To Call Men to Christ*

• *Regularly present the gospel and invite men to put their faith in Jesus.* Offer opportunities "from the front" at thought-through intervals.

• *"Be there" for men when they feel the need.* Address their turning points and crises from the front. Enlist your strong disciples to be part of a "system" to reach out to hurting men (e.g., meet for ten minutes right after the service in Room 100 where strong disciples set coffee and breakfast appointments with men).

• *Teach your men the difference between "commitment" and "surrender."*

• *Call your men to surrender.* Tell them Dr. Rogers's story, then issue the call: "You must reach a turning point. The turning point of our lives is when we stop seeking the God (or gods) we want and start seeking the God who is. No amount of wanting to re-create Him in your imagination to be different is going to have any effect on His unchanging character and nature. Your principal task, then, is to come humbly to the foot of the cross and there surrender of your life to the lordship of Jesus Christ. If you would like to do that right now. . . " (Then lead them in a prayer of surrender that includes repentance and expresses faith.)

• *Teach them how to abide in Christ.* Teach your men how to abide. Equip them with the spiritual disciplines to "continue" in Christ all week long.

EQUIPPING MEN IN CHRIST

Second, men need to grow in their faith. A disciple is *equipped* in a process of ongoing spiritual growth and transformation—*teaching.* The second part of making disciples is teaching—to equip men to live like Christ. The church is a learning organization.

A man came to my home to fix my Internet service. He was a nice man with a good heart, but he wasn't trained to figure out my problem. The next man had the proper training and easily solved the problem. An untrained Christian is no better off than an unskilled laborer or a high school dropout. He simply won't enjoy as much of the abundant life as a man who has been discipled.

Have a Plan

It may do more harm than good to invite a man to become a Christian if we have no plan to train him how to truly know and follow Christ.

When we don't disciple (educate, train, equip) a man who professes Christ, he will almost always become lukewarm in faith, worldly in behavior, and hypocritical in witness.

The single most important thing we can do for a man once he believes is to help him change the core affections of his heart.

One day I was seemingly at the pinnacle of my spirituality. Then I saw a sensuous woman and was immediately tempted to lust. The world, the flesh, and the devil were telling me, "Jesus is not enough to make you happy. You need this lust." That was the lie.

Fortunately I was reminded that I needed only Christ. I was, by God's grace, able to reject the temptation because I wanted to express my faith in Jesus, that He is sufficient for me.

Can you look at something or someone, be tempted to lust for it, and say, "Lord Jesus, I don't really need that to be happy because I have You"? This pinpoints the profound difference between what it means to be "committed" to Jesus versus "surrendered" to Jesus.

Seek Heart Transformation

There is a sensitivity of spirit that can develop when your men are walking closely with Jesus, renewing themselves daily in the gospel through repentance and faith. The Holy Spirit speaks, and they hear.

Christianity is not about *behavior modification*; it is *heart transformation*. Rules and regulations to make a man a better Christian will not change his life. To change his life he must change the core affections of his heart. Jesus needs to become his highest and best thought in every situation.

What men need is to become disciples of Jesus, and the second thing this implies is that they need teaching, education, training, and equipping.

WHAT YOU CAN DO | *To Equip Men in Christ*

• *Help your men to slow down and examine their lives.* When your men first join you, they come tired. If men are tired, then they need rest. Unfortunately, many churches emphasize work, not rest, so ten years later their men are just as tired as they were when they joined! Your men won't be able to examine their lives until they slow down. They need to lower their "revs" so they can hear the "still, small" voice of God speak to them.

• *Equip your men with truth.* Keep in mind that all week long many of your men have had people tickling their ears. When a man comes to church, he wants some straight talk. He wants someone to hold him accountable. So give him the truth. Give him what Francis Schaeffer liked to call "true truth." At the same time remember that it's tough out there, so include some encouragement and support. Nothing lubricates a message to men more than a good laugh. It's also important not to take ourselves too seriously and lighten it up.

• *Equip your men to read the Bible on their own.* It's said that Spurgeon once lamented he could find ten men who would die for the Bible for every one who would actually read it. The Scriptures are key in this process of calling, equipping, and sending. Notice how this process is described in Paul's instruction to

Timothy: "From infancy you have known the Holy Scriptures, which are able to make you wise for salvation through faith in Christ Jesus [calling]. All Scripture is God-breathed and is useful for teaching, rebuking, correcting and training in righteousness [equipping], so that the servant of God may be thoroughly equipped for every good work [sending]" (2 Timothy 3:15–17).

SENDING MEN FOR CHRIST

Third, men need to be sent to live for Christ. Jesus prayed, "As the Father has sent me, I am sending you" (John 20:21). A disciple is *sent* to abide in Christ, love others, bear much fruit, and do good works/deeds.

A disciple is sent to abide in Christ. Jesus said, "If you hold [abide] to my teaching, *you are really my disciples.* Then you will know the truth, and the truth will set you free" (John 8:31–32, emphasis added).

A disciple is sent to love. "A new command I give you: Love one another. As I have loved you, so you must love one another. *By this everyone will know that you are my disciples,* if you love one another (John 13:34–35, emphasis added).

Prepare Your Men for Fruitful Lives

A disciple is sent to lead a fruitful life. Every man wants to give his life to a cause, to make a difference—the first of the three things all men want. Men are made for the task. When we disciple a man, he will eventually want to make that difference for the glory of God. "This is to my Father's glory, that you bear much fruit, *showing yourselves to be my disciples"* (John 15:8, emphasis added).

At some point, every true believer quivers a bit when he reads John 15:8. Once the grace and love of Christ sink in, a man will feel compelled to do something to serve his Lord. Here's how Brother Lawrence expressed it: "I tell you that this sweet and loving gaze of God insensibly kindles a divine fire in the soul which is set ablaze so ardently with the love of God that one is obliged to perform exterior acts to moderate it."[4]

Why do we equip men to live like Christ? So they can enjoy Christ by knowing Him better—sure, but also "so that the servant of God may be thoroughly equipped for every good work" (2 Timothy 3:17). And that's what pastors do— equip people to do those "good works":

so Christ himself gave the apostles, the prophets, the evangelists, the pastors and teachers, to equip his people for works of service, so that the body of Christ may be built up until we all reach unity in the faith and in the knowledge of the Son of God and become mature, attaining to the whole measure of the fullness of Christ (Ephesians 4:11–13, emphasis added).

"Ordain" Your Men

Once a man has been with Christ and experienced the joy of His grace, the warmth of His love, the cleansing of His forgiveness, and the indwelling of His Spirit, he inevitably comes to a point when he can no longer be happy unless he is serving the Lord.

I once met a man who said, "All my life I wanted to be a high school math teacher. Finally, my dream came true. But I soon saw two problems. First, my students were coming to class with problems math can't solve. Second, the Christian teachers in my school didn't know each other. God put a vision in my mind about how to address those two issues. *I am an ordained math teacher.*"

He understood that every vocation is holy to the Lord. Some of your men are ordained truck drivers. Some are ordained computer programmers. Others are ordained farmers. Help your men understand what they have been "ordained" to do and they will forever be grateful to you. It will completely change their view of work.

All men want to be happy. A man will feel most happy, most alive, and most useful when he is doing what he was created to do—when he finds his cause, his woman, and his God.

Besides, if you don't give him the opportunity, he will go somewhere else. Don't let this happen to you: "I was bursting at the seams to serve, but they couldn't figure out how to mobilize me."

WHAT YOU CAN DO | *To Send Men for Christ*

Help your men understand what it means to be a disciple after they leave the church building:

• *Encourage them to love like Christ.* Show them concrete ways to love others in practical ways. Wouldn't most problems go away if your men simply practiced the Golden Rule?

• *Prepare, challenge, and "ordain" them for works of service.* Give your men tasks. Once a man gets turned on to serve, he will not rest until he finds an outlet for his passion. When he comes to you, I suggest you drop everything and engage him. If you do not give such a man a place to serve, he will still find a place to serve—but it will be elsewhere. When all the time and energy to bring the man to this point are considered, I think the best course of action is to suspend all other activity until you have engaged the man in a ministry of the church. Again, if you don't, someone else will. This is an "urgent" felt need of the man.

MOVING TOWARD HEART CHANGE

Our main task is to present the gospel of Jesus in such a way that it helps men change the core affections of their hearts so they want to be disciples. Discipleship is not merely presenting *the right information* through teaching and preaching—although that is important. Discipleship includes everything that moves men along toward spiritual maturity.

How do we do that? It could be a sermon, an encouraging or inspiring word in the hall, an unforgettable solo, getting a cup of coffee together, a Sunday school lesson, a home Bible study, a hug, a small-group experience. It also includes acts of service, such as teaching Sunday school, volunteering to work in the homeless shelter, leading someone to Christ, giving or getting a meal when sick, or setting up chairs for the mission conference—anything that moves a man forward in Christ.

Build around relationships, not programs. Discipleship is more relationship than task. Love them from the front, but then get them into "life on life" groups of all kinds (e.g., home groups, couples' groups, men's groups).

Jesus is our model for making disciples. From a learning theory perspective, Jesus was a genius. His methods overlapped. He gathered men together. He forged relationships with them. They did "life" together. They dialogued. They socialized. They went with Him. They listened to His teachings. They observed His life. He gave them assignments to build their confidence and build His kingdom.

Jesus pastored for "life change." Jesus wasn't so much interested in what men heard, but how they responded. The result? Two thousand years later Christianity is the world's largest movement, and Jesus is the most famous person on earth.

POINTS TO REMEMBER

- We can give men what they really need if, instead of looking at the data, we ask God for direction.
- What men need is to become disciples of our Lord and Savior Jesus Christ and all that this implies.
- A disciple is someone *called* to live "in" Christ, *equipped* to live "like" Christ, and *sent* to live "for" Christ.
- To be truly happy a man must be born again—to surrender his life to Jesus.
- An untrained Christian is no better off than an unskilled laborer or a high school dropout. He simply won't enjoy as much of the abundant life as a man who has been discipled.
- The single most important thing we can do for a man once he believes is to help him change the core affections of his heart.
- Once the grace and love of Christ sink in, a man will feel compelled to do something to serve his Lord.
- Help your men understand what they have been "ordained" to do and they will forever be grateful to you.
- Jesus is our model for making disciples. From a learning theory perspective, Jesus was a genius.

HOW I BECAME A DISCIPLE
—A CASE STUDY

In this chapter, I want to illustrate the calling, sending, and equipping of one man—me. You will quickly see my equipping and sending did not occur in a linear, step-by-step process. I think that's an important point to make. Like most men, my discipleship has been fluid, dynamic, and organic.

Since I was a little boy until now, I have never belonged to a church that had a "separate" men's ministry program or organization (although they encouraged life-on-life men's small groups). You don't *have* to have a separate ministry to men to disciple men. I think that's another important point to make. In fact, my most important discipleship took place in a couples' group.

There is a "compounding" nature to discipleship. It is through repetitive exposures to the "same" ideas that the truth slowly but surely takes hold. For example, the first time the disciples experienced Jesus calming the storm, they said, "What kind of man is this? Even the winds and the waves obey Him!" (Matthew 8:27). The second time He did it they declared, "Truly you are the Son of God," and they worshiped Him (Matthew 14:33).

When the space shuttle was in orbit, it wanted to veer off course about 90 percent of the time. Many small rockets and thrusters regularly fired to keep the shuttle on its correct orbital course. A lot of men are like the space shuttle. They veer off course a great deal of the time. Like those small rockets and thrusters, steady discipleship can direct a man's life to the right course.

PRAISE FOR DISCIPLE-MAKING CHURCHES

I praise God for the churches where I was discipled as a young man. In one of the churches, I recall Pastor Chuck Green. When Dr. Green preached, he preached to men. Of course, he preached to women too, but he was a man's man. He used a lot of humor and stories that I could relate to as a man. I didn't feel like Christianity was for wimps. He had a vision to make disciples—calling, equipping, and sending.

When Chuck was seventeen, he was paralyzed in a trampoline accident. He eventually regained enough use of his legs to shuffle along, scraping his feet as he walked with the aid of a cane. I think his courage inspired me more than I realized at the time.

That's the church where both of our children answered the "call" to become Christians and were baptized. In concert with our parental training, that's where they were "equipped" through the youth programs and Sunday school classes. They also attended elementary through high school in our church's affiliated Christian school.

When our children were "sent" to college, they both lived out their faith and joined local churches. When they married, our church performed the weddings.

After twenty-five years at our church, my wife, Patsy, and I were called back to a former church. At the exit interview with our existing pastor, he asked if I had any advice to offer. I said, "Not really. You're doing great. Keep doing what you're doing. You're attracting lots of young families.

"But one thing I do encourage you to remember: I am the product. I am what this church produces. I am the goal. I represent success. All the programs are great, but only to the extent that they make disciples—just like you did for me."

GROWING UP IN CHURCH

I grew up in a church that baptized me as a child, taught Bible stories, had confirmation classes, allowed me to be an altar boy, and offered youth group meetings, which I attended.

Growing up in the church, I assumed I was "in." Jesus was my example. I believed what I was told. However, I was not taught that I was a sinner in need of personal spiritual transformation. I have no recollection of any teaching that I needed a Savior, or that Jesus wanted to have a relationship with me to help guide my life. I'm not saying the gospel was not preached, only that I have no such recollection. My parents and three brothers had the same experience.

Religion for me was veneration of a majestic historical figure but with no present relevance or personal application. I believed in a God I did not understand and lived in a world that I had no reason to think He inhabited.

SEARCHING FOR MEANING AND PURPOSE

Like all young men, I wanted my life to count. I was searching for meaning and purpose. Once I kept reading, repeating, and studying a prayer to conjure up a "feeling" of connection to God, which never came.

As a high schooler, a voice inside my head kept screaming, "You were created for a purpose!" But everything in my life bored me—school, my part-time job, my family. I even bored myself. I was angry that life seemed so "little," so insignificant, and so pointless.

I had no idea who I was, why I existed, where I was going, or how to get there. My world didn't work, so I quit high school in the middle of my senior year.

The next thing I remember it was 5:00 a.m. at Fort Benning, Georgia, and a ferocious drill sergeant was screaming for me to get out of bed for a three-mile run before breakfast. After several months of training, I was assigned to the 82nd Airborne Division at Fort Bragg, North Carolina.

The structure and boundaries of the army actually created a sense of safety for me. After passing the GED test, I enrolled in night classes at NC State University's Fort Bragg branch campus. I was still searching. For an English literature class, I read in *Hamlet*, "This above all: to thine own self be true and it must follow as the night the day, thou canst not then be false to any man."

I thought, *That's the most noble thought I have ever heard uttered!* I adopted it as my life credo and said, "I will always try to do the right thing by everyone I meet." Essentially, on that day I became a *moralist.* I thought I had broken the code.

However, feelings of loneliness soon overwhelmed me. I still wondered, "Can God help me?" A fellow soldier invited me to a church in nearby Fayetteville. They allowed me to be an assistant to the couple leading the high school youth group. The relationships filled a void, but only part of it.

I set an appointment with the pastor and, with tears streaming down my face, told him how lonely and sad I was. He smiled and said, "You will get over this. It's just something we all have to go through from time to time." I left his office knowing that we both were lost.

Having failed to find meaning and purpose in religion, after the army and college I decided to try my hand at business. I became a *materialist* in addition to a moralist. Soon I was meeting all my goals, but the more I achieved the more miserable I became. Life was futile.

THE PAIN LEADING UP TO NEW BIRTH

In the meantime, I had met Patsy. She wanted to marry a Christian, so I convinced her I was one. Within weeks of our marriage, however, it was obvious that we had an ambiguity of terms about what it meant to be a Christian.

I thought being a Christian meant "living by a set of Christian values." I was surprised to learn that for Patsy being a Christian meant "a personal relationship with Jesus grounded in faith." I thought it was a *task*—something I did to make God happy (or at least avoid His wrath). But for Patsy it was a *relationship*—a love relationship in which God actively guided her daily life.

I wanted what she had. But I didn't want to give up anything to get it. So I tried to "imitate" her while living as I had always done. The harder I tried, the worse things became. One dreary day I came home from work in my new luxury car, closed the garage door, then tried to knock down the garage wall with the sole of my foot for ten minutes or so. The angst was eating a hole through me.

Sunday morning I said to Patsy, "Let's go to church." At this point, I was blaming my wife for my miseries and thought, *If we go to church maybe it will help Patsy, and I might meet some investors for my real estate deals.*

After the service, several young couples surrounded us in the most pleasant way—like they really cared. Two of the husbands took a personal interest in me. We went to lunch. We talked. We went to their homes for dinners. They invited us to a Friday night Bible study that met in the home of an optometrist and his wife.

I tried—I really did. I wanted to perform. I wanted to make them happy. I wanted to be like them. I did my best. But I couldn't. I was selfish and, worse, pretended that I was not.

Waves of frustration swept over me. One morning I was ranting and raving, trying to expel my pain by taking these frustrations out on my wife. I said things to her that a man should never say to a woman. With tears rolling down her face, she just sat there and "took it like a man."

When my rage was winding down, our eyes met and I was transfixed. I wanted to look away, but I couldn't. After she held my gaze for what seemed like a brief eternity, she asked, "Pat, is there *anything* about me that you like?"

I wandered off to my office and spent the morning staring out my window. I wondered, "What happened to you, Morley? You wanted your life to count, to make a difference. But you're just a nobody headed nowhere." And it was true.

I had taken one step forward, but then two steps back. It was time for another try at "religion."

CONVICTION OF SIN AT SUNDAY SCHOOL

We started to attend a Sunday school class for young couples led by a wonderful middle-aged couple. It was a case of "equipping" before the "calling" had taken place! The man read from Ephesians 5:25–33. I only remember the first few words: "Husbands, love your wives, just as Christ loved the church and gave himself up for her to make her holy."

At the particular moment he read, I was staring at the floor. My face flushed and I started sweating profusely. Within a minute or so my undershirt was soaked. I have never felt more embarrassed in my life. I was certain that everyone knew that I was not loving my wife as I should. I was sure they were all now staring at me. I couldn't look up—I didn't want to. A powerful force of true moral guilt swept over me. It was the first time I recall feeling what I later came to understand was conviction of sin. But I didn't know what to do with it. I soldiered on.

THE CALL TO SURRENDER

In his sermons, the pastor was telling me about Jesus in a way I had never considered—a personal God interested in me personally.

As we drove away from church one Sunday in August 1973, I was picking on Patsy for something I cannot now remember. Something inside of me snapped. I finally came to the end of myself. I pulled out my white handkerchief and surrendered. I prayed, "God, I just can't do this anymore. I'm a sinful man, and I need You to save me. Jesus, I surrender my life to You, and ask You to come into my life and change me." I have never been the same.

Of course, every man's story is different in the details. But in another sense every man's story is the same: the feelings . . . the futility . . . the pain . . . the lashing out . . . the drawing toward Jesus . . . the witnesses . . . the "hearing" of God's Word . . . the conviction of sin . . . the preaching of God's Word . . . the coming to an end of self.

Fortunately for me (and for my wife, children, parents, and brothers), our church had a vision to disciple me to become a godly man, husband, and father. The pastor was *determined* to make this happen. And the church had adopted a *strategy* that not only got me started, but had additional steps to *sustain* my growth and service.

And best of all—at least for me—our church acted quickly once they learned I had received Christ.

A DISCIPLE EQUIPPED
Through Study, Memorization, and Reading of the Bible
I've had so many awesome opportunities to grow, but the most systematic and comprehensive one came when Patsy and I were invited to join a home Bible study led by Jim Gillean. Jim was an engineer who really made us all think about what the Scriptures meant and, importantly, how they applied to everyday life.

During those Bible studies I learned how to read the Bible for myself, how to pray, and how to have a daily devotional.

Here was an essential key to success: The group was small enough that we each got to know and care about each other personally. I was not just one among many. What I thought was important on every issue or question, every time. Because the group was small, we became honest and vulnerable as we learned to trust each other—the essense of "life on life"—something that doesn't happen when groups get large. There's an inverse relationship between spiritual transformation and the size of the group: the smaller the group, the greater the impact people have on each other. That's the math of discipleship.

Scripture memorization was popular at the time, and I memorized hundreds of verses—one of the best "equip" things I ever did. I still recall verses every day that I learned back then.

At a weekend seminar, the speaker noted the book of Proverbs has 31 chapters. He suggested we read one chapter a day each month. I took the challenge and for fifteen years or so, I read a chapter in Proverbs every day. With that kind of exposure, I was soon quoting "Proverbs" in my everyday language.

To Be Sent

We were invited into Jim's Bible study as part of a package to both "equip" and "send" us. We were "sent" when they asked Patsy and me to lead a six-week Sunday school class for new Christians that repeated several times a year. Part of the deal was that all the pastors and lay leaders for evangelism, new Christian training, and home Bible studies met once a week to be "equipped" in our own Bible study.

Leading the class for new Christians was definitely "learning by doing." Even though the new believers' questions were simple and basic, I still had to scramble because I was a rookie at serving Christ. Leading helped me grow like a weed.

To Evangelize

Our church hosted a Campus Crusade for Christ weekend training to teach people how to do personal evangelism. Patsy and I attended, and I just ate it up. They "equipped" us on Saturday and "sent" us on Sunday! I led my first person to Jesus on a Sunday afternoon home visit.

I started taking businessmen to lunch, sharing my testimony, and asking, "Where are you on your spiritual pilgrimage?" If they didn't understand the gospel, I would read them Campus Crusade's Four Spiritual Laws, and most of them became Christians too.

SENT INTO THE MARKETPLACE

Six of us in the business community started meeting in a weekly small group to share, learn, and pray for each other. Howard Dayton, who later founded Crown Ministries (now Compass—Finances God's Way) would come each week with first drafts of the material that would eventually become the Crown course. He asked our opinions but, of course, we didn't have much to say because most of us were pretty young in our faith and knowledge. The main thing about this group was that we were "for" each other, and that "equipped" me to have adult male friendships for the first time.

One day I proposed to our small group that we fan out in the community and take positions in politics, education, and civic life. I volunteered to take the "civic life" category and joined the Winter Park Chamber of Commerce. They immediately put me on the Program Committee, and six months later I was the chairperson. I prayed, "God, why am I here?" I sensed God had "sent" me there to start a prayer breakfast, so I acted.

Just before Thanksgiving 1978, the Chamber hosted its first Prayer Breakfast with about 150 people attending. Several received Christ. The Chamber is no longer involved but the Leadership Prayer Breakfast is still going strong, and hundreds of business leaders have become Christians as a result.

A CHALLENGING TIME
OF EQUIPPING AND SENDING

About the time of the first prayer breakfast, someone invited me to attend a weekend men-only retreat hosted by The Fellowship at Windy Gap, North Carolina.

The main speaker was Tom Skinner, evangelist and former gang member. Tom's messages focused on the kingdom of God, loving God, and loving other people—especially people who are different from us. It was the first time I can remember "hearing" that I didn't have to work myself into a stupor to earn God's approval and love (although I have no doubt the words had been spoken to me before—it was just my time). It was also the first time I remember being challenged to love people outside my comfort zone.

Tom liked to play tennis, and they had courts at Windy Gap. The next night I skipped out on the main session and walked up to the courts. Tom was there hitting balls. We struck up a conversation. He talked to me as though I was the only person on Earth still living. I felt the love of God coming through him into me. It was a supreme "equipping" time for me.

Sent to Start Leadership Conferences

Being the task-oriented man I was, I immediately asked Tom if he would come to Orlando and share his message with all my tired, worn-out Christian friends. He said yes, and soon we hosted the first of several Christian Leadership Conferences in Orlando. I remember my Christian workaholic friends coming up to Tom after his sessions with tears streaming down their faces.

One man said, "I feel such relief. I have been under such a heavy burden. I just always felt like I needed to do more and more to please God. I was afraid that I was leaving something undone. For the first time I realize that what He wants most is a relationship with me—to love me and make me a whole man."

Sent to Start a One-on-One Friendship

One thing Tom said that weekend at Windy Gap gripped me: "If you want to change your city or church, don't try to organize a big revival. Instead, find some like-minded men and become to each other what you want your city or church to become. Meet together and share your lives with each other. That will create a model so attractive that others will want to be part of it." That really grabbed hold of my insides.

As soon as I returned home, I started praying for God to send me a man. On the following Sunday, I saw Ken Moar, a friendly man thirty years my senior. He agreed to meet with me once a week. We sought to become to each other what we wanted our church and community to become. We met weekly for thirty-two years until he passed away, and virtually everything I've ever done in ministry was first discussed with Ken, including The Man in the Mirror Bible Study, and the Man in the Mirror ministry.

SENT TO SERVE IN THE COMMUNITY

Talking with Merthie

In 1980, here in Orlando, we had a racially charged civil disturbance that was big enough to make the evening network news. I went home for lunch and, that day, our African American housekeeper, Merthie, was there. It was awkward. I finally found these words coming out of my mouth, "Merthie, how long do you think it will be before we are able to be right with each other?"

She said, "Oh, I don't know."

"Well, Merthie, what keeps you going—what is your hope?"

She said, "Oh, I don't know."

I said, "Merthie, do you think we will ever get by all of this, and learn to live together as Christians?"

"Oh, I don't know," she said once again.

I went into my home office and began to sob. I thought, *I am a Christian. I need to do something to respond to this.*

Taking a First Step

Eventually, with the input of an African American college professor that I knew fairly well and motivated by my relationship with Tom Skinner, I convened a meeting of black and white men—not to change Orlando, but to become to each other what we think Orlando should become.

I made a list of twenty white men, and the professor made a list of twenty black men. We invited them to come to a Saturday morning meeting. Half came—ten black and ten white. At the meeting, there was disagreement about the first step. As it turned out, exactly half of the black men wanted to do a task and the other half wanted to do relationships. And exactly half of the white men wanted to do a task and the other half wanted to do relationships.

It should be clear that this is not an ethnic issue. It is a human issue. Some men are wired for task and some are wired for relationship. But because I was under the influence of Tom Skinner, I exerted my will to take the "relationship precedes task" approach.

We met one Saturday morning each month for the next five years. We called ourselves "The Black/White Fellowship."

Interestingly, more tasks and "sending" came out of that group than you can imagine: men going to seminary, starting ministries, meeting financial needs, helping the poor, fixing houses, assisting with medical needs.

God "sent" me to lead The Black/White Fellowship, but He used my relationship with Merthie to inspire me to go. I'm also pretty sure this would never have happened if I hadn't met Tom. As Tom liked to say, "A relationship is the most powerful force in the world."

BEING EQUIPPED ALONG

The equipping part of discipleship can be programmatic and linear, like through Sunday school, adult learning classes, a small-group curriculum, or a preaching series. A lot of discipleship, though, just "happens" as we intersect with people, ideas, and opportunities. Here are some of the ways I've been equipped that don't fit neatly onto a timeline.

Through Christian Books

As the author of twenty books, I've seen up close the power and impact of Christian literature. I have repeatedly seen how a man will get hold of a book, and then God will use the book to get hold of the man. As a visual learner, reading Christian literature has been for me one of the most powerful ways I've been equipped. Christian literature began affecting me early. Frankly, though, some of the early books I read were too advanced for me. I just didn't have the theological vocabulary I have today. But I soldiered on, and several authors left deep imprints on my faith and worldview—men like Francis Schaeffer, J. I. Packer, Oswald Chambers, and C. S. Lewis. But all these authors were much too dense for me in the beginning.

For Parenting

Nothing could be more important for a man with children than to be equipped as a godly father. As we started our own family, a very attractive couple in our church who raised four successful boys invited us to attend a parenting class. We already knew about the class, but the clincher for us to attend was a personal invitation to me from the man. I felt honored to be asked personally by a leader in the church.

I had never been methodically "equipped" in the area of parenting. My wife, Patsy, had handed me many pages and even chapters of great parenting books to read—Dobson mostly. However, listening to our teachers and comparing notes with our peers brought everything down to street level.

A TRANSITION INTO MINISTRY

Some of your men will be called to lead. Some will even enter ministry as I did in 1991. I won't tell you all the details of my "sending" into ministry, but several preludes are worth a mention.

First, I became bi-vocational. I didn't have this category in my vocabulary at the time, but I was spending more and more of my time doing ministry and leaving the business to others.

After The Black/White Fellowship my wife and I became the host couple for Campus Crusade's Executive Ministries in Orlando. In the last half of the 1980s we hosted evangelistic dinner parties and small follow-up dinners in our home. We saw dozens of business leaders and their spouses profess faith.

I started The Man in the Mirror Bible Study in 1986. The concept was to have a place to "equip" the businessmen "called" through the outreach dinners. As it turned out, none of those men ever attended, but a whole different group of business types showed up. And our involvement with Executive Ministries led to a host of other ministries.

In 1989 Reformed Theological Seminary started a campus in Orlando, and my company did the real estate work. I was intrigued, so I started taking classes.

R. C. Sproul and other great professors opened my eyes to a whole new world of theology, Christian history, and so much more.

Also in 1989, I wrote *The Man in the Mirror.* By 1991, there just wasn't enough time to do it all, so I left business and started the ministry, Man in the Mirror.

TO LIVE FOR CHRIST

Each of your men is unique and God deals with them as individuals. Nevertheless, all men need to be called to live in Christ, equipped to live like Christ, and sent to live for Christ. I hope this case study creates a sense of freedom and variety about the many ways your men can become disciples of Jesus.

POINTS TO REMEMBER

- There is a "compounding" nature to discipleship. It is through repetitive exposures to the "same" ideas that the truth slowly but surely takes hold.
- "I am the product. All the programs are great, but only to the extent that they make disciples—just like you did for me."
- When Dr. Chuck Green preached, he preached to men. He was a man's man and used stories that I could relate to as a man. I didn't feel like Christianity was for wimps. He had a vision to make disciples—calling, equipping, and sending.
- I thought Christianity was a *task*—something I did to make God happy (or at least avoid His wrath). But for Patsy it was a *relationship*—a love relationship in which God actively guided her daily life.
- I tried—I really did. I wanted to perform. I wanted to make them happy. I wanted to be like them. I did my best. But I couldn't. I was selfish and, worse, pretended that I was not.
- In his sermons, the pastor was telling me about Jesus in a way I had never considered—a personal God interested in me personally.
- I've had so many awesome opportunities to grow, but the most systematic and comprehensive one came when Patsy and I were invited to join a home Bible study.

SUCCESS FACTORS
IN DISCIPLING MEN

What are the factors that lead to effective discipling of men? In chapters 7 and 8 I want to show you what research has revealed about churches that are effectively pastoring men—nine major themes and their related success factors.

As mentioned in chapter 1, several years ago I was alarmed at how many highly capable, willing, and proven pastors (and laymen) had burned out on men's discipleship. They simply did not know how to sustain their ministries to men. Yet others were flourishing.

In 2002 I decided to study this problem academically by pursuing a PhD in management. I wanted to understand, "Why do some churches succeed at men's discipleship while others languish or fail?" What were the successful pastors doing differently from the pastors of the ineffective or failed ministries to men?

I do not believe the actions of the Holy Spirit are limited by research studies, but research can clarify what's working for others. The Spirit usually does His best work when people know what they're doing—whether it's piloting an airplane, performing surgery, programming a computer, selling a car, managing a company, or pastoring men.

My first step was to understand what scholarly management literature had to say about sustaining change and the implementation factors that lead to success. I was amazed at how rich and diverse the literature is for businesses, while churches as organizations have been sorely neglected. Many well-known, proven concepts have simply not migrated to churches where new "wineskins" are needed.

THIS IS REALLY IMPORTANT: THE PROBLEM WITH INTRODUCING CHANGE

I quickly discovered that the odds of *any* new initiative succeeding are quite low. Only about one-third of all organizational initiatives succeed, and that's regardless of sector—whether public, private, or nonprofit. Shockingly, 67 percent fail outright,[1] while up to 70 percent of all new products fail.[2] Only 44 percent of new business start-ups succeed beyond four years.[3]

Research shows that, all things being equal, most of your new initiatives will never get past the idea stage and, of those that do, two-thirds will fail. But things don't have to be equal!

You can dramatically improve your own results by knowing what works. All truth is God's truth, and the truth about implementing and sustaining change has been thoroughly studied and documented in management literature over the last one hundred years. By the end of this and the next chapter, you will have a research-based snapshot of what works in churches that have effective men's discipleship ministries. And in chapter 9, I'll pull all these variables into a highly adaptable model that you can use to implement, and sustain, the most effective possible men's discipleship initiative for your church.

OVERVIEW: THE THREE MAIN FACTORS

Many variables have to be in place to succeed, and we'll get into them shortly. But first, my research clearly identified three main factors that tower over the others. If you focus on these three, you will for the most part find that everything falls into place:

- *Vision*: a vision to disciple *every* man in the church.
- *Determination*: a personally involved pastor who is determined that men's discipleship will work "no matter what."
- *Sustainable strategy*: a "sustainable" strategy to move men forward as disciples.

The Big Three

First, success hinges on having a vision to disciple every man in your church. In the effective churches, the senior pastors had a clear vision and a passionate commitment to disciple every man in their churches. And they "sold" their visions hard yet were patient about giving people time to get on board. The research revealed it is clearly not enough for a layman or even an associate pastor to have this vision. That's not to say men won't be discipled if the senior pastor is not on board, but the results will be a fraction of what they could have been. In the ineffective churches, the senior pastors did not see men's discipleship as a top priority.

Second, you must be "determined" to make men's discipleship work. The most striking finding was the level of personal involvement by the successful senior pastors. This is not to say that the senior pastor has to do everything. In the successful churches other pastors or laymen often did the work—but the senior pastor never fully let go. They viewed themselves as the ongoing champions for men's discipleship. That stood in sharp contrast to their counterparts in the ineffective and failed programs. The word that best captures the will of the pastor to see it through is "determination." But determination is not a strategy, which leads us to the other main factor.

Third, successful men's discipleship depends on having a strategy to sustain your efforts. "Sustainability" easily ranks as the number one problem in men's discipleship ministry. Many churches find it easy to start men's discipleship, but then it fizzles. It's the proverbial roller-coaster effect. In the effective churches, the senior pastors had a planning model, method, or process (not just a curriculum) they employed to not only create discipleship momentum, but also to sustain it. They discovered an organized way to sustain discipleship—their determination was not in vain. However, the ineffective and failed churches created a lot of momentum from time to time, but had no strategy to keep it going.

What Is a Strategy?

I want to be very careful about the use of the word *strategy*. For our purposes, the concept is more important than the word. By the word *strategy* we're talking about "a sustainable way to get men's discipleship done long term."

Again, people often use different words to mean the same thing, and the same words to mean different things. You may prefer *strategy, system, model, method, process, program, plan,* or some other word. I don't want us to get hung up on words. *Webster's Online Dictionary* defines these terms in a way that suggests they're all getting at the same thing—an organized way to achieve a desired outcome:

- Strategy: An elaborate and systematic plan of action.
- System: A procedure or process for obtaining an objective.
- Model: A simplified description of a complex entity or process.
- Method: A way of doing something, especially a systematic one; implies an orderly, logical arrangement (usually in steps).
- Process: A particular course of action intended to achieve a result.
- Program: A series of steps to be carried out or goals to be accomplished.
- Plan: A series of steps to be carried out or goals to be accomplished.

As you can see, there's a lot of overlap.

Developing a strategy is a learnable skill. By the end of this and the next two chapters, you will have the essentials of a sustainable men's discipleship strategy.

Our model for this is Jesus. His *vision* was to seek and to save the lost. His *determination* ranged from clearing the temple to His submissive prayer in the garden of Gethsemane. His *sustainable strategy* was training disciples to train other disciples. As already mentioned, all the factors that follow are important, of course, but when these three are in place the others appear to follow in the course of time.

Vision. Determination. Sustainable strategy. Keep these three in mind as you read about the nine essential themes and related success factors. Each theme will include findings from research literature, biblical corroboration from Nehemiah, and an example of the theme in action.

Now back to the bigger picture.

NINE ESSENTIAL THEMES FOR SUCCESS

Once I understood the success factors from the literature, I designed an inductive, multiple-case study to investigate the presence or absence of those factors in churches that have been successful and unsuccessful in implementing men's discipleship.

I was able to organize the success factors I found into nine essential themes:

1. Leadership
2. Vision
3. People
4. Planning
5. Resources
6. Execution
7. Communication Plan
8. Resistance
9. Sustainability

Ironically, the themes I discovered can all be found by reading the book of Nehemiah—written nearly 2,500 years ago! I wasn't surprised. (More on Nehemiah as we go.)

I have memorized these nine themes. Whenever I have a problem, I run through the list. That helps me locate and clarify the problem.

There is no secret knowledge. We are not doomed to repeat the mistakes of the past. However, that doesn't mean this knowledge is lying on top of the ground like nuggets of gold. It must be mined. So let's dig in. We'll cover the first four themes in this chapter, and the other five in the next.

Incidentally, these findings can be generalized to help you in other areas of your church and ministry—or any organization.

THEME 1: LEADERSHIP

Bill Bright, founder of Cru, frequently said, "Everything boils down to leadership." All the research ever recorded concludes that you can't launch a broad and extended change initiative, program, or process under the leadership of middle managers. Even Jesus launched His kingdom through personal involvement.

The research is quite clear: The senior pastor is the key to men's discipleship. He doesn't have to do it all, but he does have to make "men's discipleship" into a genuine priority that the whole church understands and adopts.

Unquestionably, instability and turnover in key leadership positions always hurts momentum. Football teams and NASCAR teams come to mind.

Implementation Factors from the Literature
Research studies in the literature found the following factors necessary for effective leadership:

- Personal involvement of the senior leader in the change initiative
- Commitment to long-term results (determination)
- Transformational style
- Organization-wide support from the CEO, the senior or top management, the implementation team, the champion, and the implementing managers

Biblical Corroboration in Nehemiah

Nehemiah 1 portrays a man who weeps, mourns, fasts, prays, and repents for his people—a humble man. Jim Collins, author of the bestseller *Good to Great*, found that leaders of great companies were a mixture of personal humility and professional will—what he termed a "Level 5" leader.[4] The rest of the book of Nehemiah presents a case study of a transformational leader with an iron will who was personally involved in making his vision become reality. And Nehemiah found support from his CEO, the king. Nehemiah said, "Let him send me to the city in Judah where my ancestors are buried so that I can rebuild it" (Nehemiah 2:5), and the king granted his request.

An Example of Leadership

Dr. Pete Alwinson was, for twenty-six years, the senior pastor of Willow Creek Church, a Presbyterian church in Winter Springs, Florida. Pete actually started his church with a men's Bible study that met on Tuesday mornings. The church grew to a congregation of eight hundred on Sunday mornings.

Pete put his money where his mouth was when it came to men's discipleship. Every week he scheduled three men for breakfast or lunch to get to know them better, understand their needs, and pray for them. And he didn't let the men pick up the check! For Pete, the relationship *was* the task.

He also taught men's Bible studies. He personally conducted the annual elder training. And he participated in an annual men's wilderness adventure—as one of the guys.

When I asked him to rate his commitment and involvement to implement his men's discipleship program, he said, "Well, I'd say it's 100 percent. I'm 100 percent committed to this. Our church started from a men's ministry. The main thing I do is develop men." Later he added, "I believe as it goes with the men of the church, so goes the church." That kind of passionate commitment attracts men.

WHAT YOU CAN DO | *To Promote Leadership*

• Be firmly committed to not only support but to be personally involved in both the initial implementation and the ongoing execution until sustainability is reached—let's call this "determination."

• Encourage the senior church staff, including lay leaders, to believe in the program, because they are needed to help build organization-wide commitment. Any church staff involved in implementing the program must also be committed to long-term success. A program champion who is capable and committed will need to recruit a team of like-minded individuals.

THEME 2: VISION

The second success theme, vision, was a powerful factor found in each of the case-study churches. The leaders and people developed strategies, plans, and resources that clearly followed the senior pastor's vision.

Vision is more powerful than labor. Vision sets forces in motion that, once released, can no longer be contained. Consider these visionary statements, all of which reached or are approaching fulfillment:

• "We will put a man on the moon by the end of the decade."—President John Kennedy
• "To organize the world's information and make it universally accessible and useful."—Google's mission statement
• "Imagine a world in which every single person on the planet is given free access to the sum of all human knowledge."—the founder of Wikipedia
• "A computer on every desk and in every home."—Bill Gates, retired chairman of Microsoft
• "I want to make it possible during my lifetime for anyone in the world to taste a Coke."—the CEO of Coca-Cola in the 1950s
• "If we're going to be nationwide, then we need batteries in every place in America that sells batteries."—Norm Miller, then-chairman of Interstate Batteries, in 1978

It would be difficult to overstate the power of a well-formed vision statement. For example, today you can go to any city in America with a population of one thousand or more people and buy an Interstate battery. To put a vision in "just the right words in just the right order" can enflame people's imaginations and commitment. One great idea can change the world.

Implementation Factors from the Literature

Research studies in the literature found the following factors necessary for effective vision:

- The gathering and analysis of information
- The creation of a clear and compelling vision
- The creation of a sense of urgency for change
- The introduction of an initiative that works and is perceived to work

Biblical Corroboration in Nehemiah

After Nehemiah had gathered information from his brother (1:3), he prayerfully thought about it (1:4–11). God put a vision into his mind to rebuild the city of his fathers (2:5). He first shared his vision with the king (2:4–5). Once he arrived in Jerusalem, he secretly surveyed the damage under cover of darkness (2:11–16). When he introduced his vision and plan, it captured the imaginations of the leaders in Jerusalem. They believed his plan would work! (2:17–18).

Two Examples of Vision

At Willow Creek Church, the motto of Dr. Alwinson from the start was "No man left behind." It's crystal clear, reflects a sense of urgency, and inspired a large following.

His vision and goal was for *every* man in his church to be discipled. The results are pretty amazing: 95 percent of his men professed faith in Christ, 75 percent were engaged in spiritual growth, and 75 percent were serving the Lord in some capacity.

The vision of Tom Lipsey, senior pastor of Montgomery Community Church in Cincinnati, was "to see every man in the church become a radical follower of God, very devoted and effective in his family, doing life together in accountable relationships with other men, and sending them out in mission whether at work, home, or in the community." In others words, the vision is to make disciples of as many men as possible. That's especially significant since men's discipleship was not a priority when he arrived.

Both of these successful pastors see men's discipleship as the key to building strong men, marriages, families, churches, and communities. They are passionate about their visions, which helped them foster church-wide commitment.

Ironically, neither could articulate specific goals they had for their men's discipleship programs! But they were guided by an urgent vision to disciple every man in their churches.

In fact, they depended on their visions to "catch on" and mobilize the resources of their churches to make disciples of men. They tended to use their influence rather than positional power to build support.

However, neither of these pastors neglected their other programs. But it did mean that when resources were inadequate, the men's discipleship programs did not suffer.

WHAT YOU CAN DO │ *To Bring About Vision*

- Gather and analyze information that points to the problem, need, and opportunity—information that will challenge and inspire your leaders to action. You can use statistics and points from part 1: "Understand Your Men" to create a vision.

- Develop an *all-inclusive mindset*. Traditionally, when asked, "How many men are in your men's ministry?" a pastor might respond, "eighteen." The "all-inclusive" mindset would say, "If we have 100 men in our church, then the size of our ministry to men is 100. The only question is whether or not we are doing a good job to disciple them."

- Create a clear, resonant, inspirational vision statement that creates a sense of urgency. The more pithy and memorable the better. The vision must seem to the leaders and people like it will work, and then it must work in practice.

Here are some examples of vision statements that capture the all-inclusive concept:

"No man left behind."

"Every man a disciple."

"A disciple-making ministry to every man."

THEME 3: PEOPLE

The third theme is "people." *People* here means people who "make disciples"—not the men who will be discipled. Jim Collins is famous for saying, "Get the right people on the bus." It's so true. One long-ball hitter is often more productive than three average people. My father-in-law has a favorite saying: "Amateurs teach amateurs to be amateurs." It's not enough to recruit men with good hearts; you also need men who have skills. Most men are not trained to make disciples nor to sustain an ongoing ministry to men.

Implementation Factors from the Literature

Research studies in the literature found the following factors necessary for finding the right people:

- *Expertise.* Recruit capable, committed people who understand what is expected from them.
- *Training.* Train those people with the skills required to implement the change.
- *Culture.* Create a culture that offers psychological safety for people to dialogue about their reservations.

Biblical Corroboration in Nehemiah

Nehemiah challenged his people with a compelling vision to rebuild the walls of Jerusalem (2:17). He created an atmosphere for people to speak up (2:18). He recruited the leaders of the city to do the work (2:16).

An Example about People

To say you need to be personally involved doesn't mean you have to do everything. Far from it. At Willow Creek, Pete empowered a leadership team to plan and execute their men's discipleship program and activities.

Pete concentrated on selling his vision to disciple every man in his church. All of Pete's lay leaders bought into his vision. That's probably because to be a leader in Pete's church, you must first have completed a special men's discipleship program that he taught and have made a commitment to the church's philosophy of developing men.

An Example of How Not to Do It

Once I spoke at an incredibly well-organized and heavily attended men's event. When the leadership team and I gathered in the pastor's study for prayer just before the event started, I noticed they all looked extremely tired. I made a mental note to look into it. Here's what I discovered later.

The senior pastor has recruited a highly capable businessman with a reputation for "getting it done" to be the event chair. The event chair then recruited a dozen other capable businessmen. Together, they put together an awesome plan to turn men out for the event.

However, after digging deeper, I learned that none of these men were very mature spiritually. In fact, they were a collection of baby Christians and cultural Christians. Since they did not have enough Christ for themselves, they really did not have enough to give away. In the process of filling the sanctuary "in the flesh," they had all gotten themselves worn down. I thought to myself, *It will be a long time before these men will ever say "Yes" again.*

WHAT YOU CAN DO | *To Have the Right People*

• Recruit capable men for every position.

• Have church policies that set priorities and allocate resources to train and support these capable men.

• Include the right people in the planning process to build a sense of ownership. They should understand what is expected from them but in a culture that allows them psychological safety to speak out and process their reservations.

THEME 4: PLANNING

It will come as no surprise that the churches effective in men's discipleship had a plan, and the others did not. What may surprise you, though, is that their plans were often (1) vague and (2) stored in the senior pastor's head.

Surprisingly, having an elaborate written plan is not an essential success factor. In an executive program I attended at the Harvard Business School for owners and presidents of smaller companies, I learned that operators of smaller enterprises often don't have written plans. That doesn't mean they don't have plans—just not in writing. Successful businessmen—and pastors—always have a plan, even if they keep it in their heads.[5] That certainly was the case in this research.

Implementation Factors from the Literature

Research studies in the literature found the following factors necessary for successful planning:

- Making the adoption decision
- Formulating strategy
- Developing concrete plans (who does what by when)

Biblical Corroboration in Nehemiah

Nehemiah made his decision and formulated his strategy while still in Persia (1:8–11). He developed a comprehensive plan to rebuild the wall once he arrived in Jerusalem and analyzed the situation (2:11–16).

An Example about Planning

Ironically, while the vision of his church was tightly focused, Pastor Alwinson described both planning and execution as "messy"—a condition not uncommon in nonprofit organizations, according to Collins.[6] "Because church work overall is messy, leadership is incredibly messy," Alwinson told me. "You are dealing with paid and volunteer staff in the church. Implementing change and leadership in that kind of a context can be extremely difficult. You don't have money or position to leverage anything," he continued. "It has to be based on relationship."

At first, the lack of written plans made things appear chaotic and disorganized. But that was not the case at all. Pete knew how to keep "men's discipleship" moving along. And his determination kept them on track.

First, they created momentum by periodically hosting men's events and activities. Second, they captured momentum by inviting attendees to join follow-up groups. Third, they sustained momentum by assimilating men into the existing ministries of the church. And they kept repeating the cycle over and over again. (This foreshadows the No Man Left Behind model I will present in chapter 9.)

WHAT YOU CAN DO | *To Promote Planning*

• Select a proven *sustainable* men's discipleship planning strategy—such as our No Man Left Behind Model. Most of the failures we observe started here— picking a model that was doomed from the start. Once all the data have been gathered and analyzed by the involved parties, the decision is made to adopt a specific model. This process proceeds slowly to give everyone time to register concerns and work out their issues.

• The strategy will suggest planning issues. Formulate a concrete plan to implement the program using the model you have selected. The concrete plans should identify who will be involved, how they will be resourced, and what the schedule will look like.

• Create an atmosphere in which people can express their reservations. The planning process needs to consider how the program will be sustained from the start (e.g., the necessity of ongoing senior pastor involvement and developing organization-wide commitment). These plans do not necessarily need to be elaborate or even written.

POINTS TO REMEMBER

• Research shows that, all things being equal, most of your new initiatives will never get past the idea stage and, of those that do, two-thirds will fail.
• You can dramatically improve your particular results by knowing what works.
• Three main success factors tower over the others:
  – *Vision*: A vision to disciple *every* man in the church
  – *Determination*: A personally involved pastor who is determined that men's discipleship will work "no matter what"
  – *Sustainable Strategy*: A "sustainable" strategy to move men forward as disciples
• Possibly the most powerful idea we have been able to develop is what we call *the "all-inclusive" mindset*: If you have 100 men in your church, then the size of your ministry to men is 100.

MORE SUCCESS FACTORS IN DISCIPLING MEN

In chapter 7 we looked at "the big three" of success factors, plus all the factors for the first four themes that need to be considered for effective men's discipleship. To complete the picture, here are the final five themes and their related success factors. Then, in the next chapter, we will tie this together into an actionable model that you can use to build a sustainable strategy to more effectively disciple *all* of your "willing" men.

THEME 5: RESOURCES

Once you have the right strategy (model) for men's discipleship, the next crucial step is to make sure you provide enough resources to see it through. My uncle Bud was a hero in the Korean War. He was a full-bird colonel in command of a tank battalion that got cut off behind enemy lines. They had advanced faster than their supply lines and got starved from the resources they needed to fight. The results were nearly catastrophic. By God's grace, Uncle Bud was able to maneuver his men back to safety. Almost every men's discipleship ministry we see is "starved" for resources.

Implementation Factors from the Literature

Research studies have found the following six resources are necessary factors to successfully implement an initiative:

- Structures: Creating organization structures (such as a committee)
- Time: Building in enough time to complete the mission
- Money: Allocating enough budget
- Expertise: Assigning staff with needed expertise
- Training: Providing training to those who need it
- Compensation: Providing rewards and incentives (monetary or non-monetary)

Biblical Corroboration in Nehemiah

Nehemiah carefully assembled the resources he would need—written authorizations (2:7), timber for construction (2:8), capable people to do the work (3:1–32), and money (7:70–72). He created an organizational structure to assign the work (3:1–32).

An Example about Resources

Harvest Community Church in Charlotte, North Carolina, started in February 1996 with five families and a vision "to develop people into followers of Jesus Christ with a passion to worship God well and communicate His love to others." In June of that year, Jeff Kisiah joined Harvest and was assigned men's discipleship as one of his responsibilities. God did some great things, but without training in a systematic approach, they experienced the typical roller coaster. In fact, after eight years only 25 percent of their men were involved in ongoing spiritual formation.

Then in 2005, Jeff sensed God's call to focus on men's discipleship. He attended our No Man Left Behind training. After learning the components of a sustainable discipleship system for men, he structured a new small-group initiative, which was launched at their annual men's event on Labor Day Weekend 2005. They call their initiative "MVP" (for Men of Valor and Prayer). By the following May, 40 percent of their men had participated at some level. By January 2007, 60 percent were participating in some disciple-making venue. By June 2008, the numbers jumped again to 75 percent involvement.

Jeff continued to involve other leaders and made sure they also received training. By mid-2008 Harvest Community Church had 350 regular attendees of which 125 were men. Of the men, 95 percent professed faith, 75 percent were involved in growth groups, and 85 percent were serving the Lord in some capacity. That's an increase in male discipleship from 25 percent to 75 percent in only three years.

WHAT YOU CAN DO | *To Allocate Resources*

- Have the planning team identify the structures, time, budget, expertise, training, and any incentives that will be needed. In the beginning, it might be a planning team of one.

- Obtain the approval and endorsement of these resources by the senior leadership or other appropriate decision-making entity.

- Include training. Training may be the most overlooked resource in men's discipleship ministry.

THEME 6: EXECUTION

In football, regardless how nice or talented a player is, he's going to be taken out of the game if he repeatedly fumbles the ball. Failure to execute loses more games than not having a good plan—at least if football coaches are to be believed. Nearly every losing football coach offers the same answer: "We just didn't execute."

If you have just the right mix of leadership, people, planning, and resources, you still have to execute. That's where the rubber meets the road.

When I built office buildings in my first career, I would marvel how on one jobsite every corner of the building would be occupied by workers. But on another jobsite, there would only be one or two subcontractors working. Invariably, the difference was in the construction foremen. Some just execute better than others. A lot of it's training, of course, but mostly it's a matter of discipline.

Implementation Factors from the Literature

Research studies in the literature found the following factors necessary for proper execution:

- Conducting pilot projects
- Implementing the change
- Getting feedback
- Making adjustments
- A contingency for taking too much time
- Obtaining systematic feedback to evaluate results

Biblical Corroboration in Nehemiah

Forty leaders and their crews worked side-by-side and shoulder-to-shoulder to rebuild the wall (3:1–32). (Today think Baptists, Methodists, Assemblies of God, Church of God, Evangelical Free, Presbyterians, Episcopalians, Catholics, nondenominationals, house churches, Pentecostals, and Methodists—all those men shoulder-to-shoulder, lifting and hauling together.) Some built large sections; others built next to where they lived. They each did according to their ability and resources.

The wall was just the pilot project Nehemiah needed for his plan to restore the nation (7:1–4). He had mechanisms in place to get feedback about progress (4:6). Nehemiah also had a contingency plan (4:16–18).

An Example of Execution

One church that has existed for thirty-six years faced serious problems when it marked its twenty-fifth anniversary. The pastor and leaders recognized the people lacked spiritual depth and commitment, and the church was not very well organized.

After concluding that classroom-style teaching had not generally produced satisfactory discipleship results, the church started an intensive one-on-one discipleship program, scheduled for sixteen weeks.

The senior pastor was the champion and involved himself every step of the way. First, he and a key layman recruited their leadership team. The team developed the implementation plan. Then they ran a pilot program parallel to the existing discipleship classes. The team gave people an opportunity to offer feedback, buy in, express reservations, and slowly get comfortable with the new program.

By taking it slowly and making adjustments along the way, they gained church-wide commitment. Then they launched the initiative for the whole congregation. They strongly encouraged every existing and new member to complete the program.

In the ten years that followed, an estimated 700 people completed the program. Attendance approximately doubled to 800. A decade later, the church was sending a number of missionaries from the congregation, it was debt free, and had 70 percent of attendees tithe—and 60 percent of those gave more than a tithe.

And there's more. People have been trained to study the Bible for themselves. The burden on the pastoral staff to shepherd and train members has decreased. It has become less likely that someone can simply drop out and not be noticed or cared about.

You may be thinking, *But this program was for both men and women.* Exactly. The mindset for ministry to men should not be *men only*, but *anything that disciples men is ministry to men.*

WHAT YOU CAN DO | *To Help Execute the Program*

• Begin with *a pilot project* that runs parallel to the existing program structures. The pilot project gives people a chance to get used to the program, debug it, attract additional support, quell resisters, and prevent major mistakes. Those tasked to implement the program are involved at all stages of planning to increase ownership and the probability of success.

• Once the pilot project demonstrates success, roll out *the discipleship program* to the entire church.

• Once the program is initially implemented, seek *feedback* through formal evaluations and maintaining a system to gather information. This will increase the likelihood of the program's success. Examples of feedback include debriefs and project audits.

• Build a contingency into the initial implementation plan. Mid-course corrections probably will be necessary to optimize the program, and several years may be required to achieve sustainability. Taking longer than expected is a typically recurring problem that should be planned for in advance.

THEME 7: COMMUNICATION PLAN

Three very different public figures all have realized the power of a good communication plan. In his autobiography, rock musician Eric Clapton revealed that during the early years of his career he shunned marketing, advertising, and publicity. He felt the purity of the music should be enough. He eventually realized his naiveté and embraced the idea that people can't acquire what they don't know about.

Billy Graham was once asked the secret of his success. He replied, "Prayer and publicity." The danger of not wanting to secularize our work is that we over-spiritualize it. We are presenting the gospel in a fallen world—a world of people who need help to hear. Dr. Graham said, "If Jesus were living on earth today, I have no doubt that His methods would be just as up-to-date as possible. Newspapers, magazines, television, the Internet, satellites—I think He would use them all to get across His message."[1]

Dwight L. Moody said, "We pray like it is all up to God. We work like it is all up to us."

To do less is to presume upon God to provide "immaculate communication."

Implementation Factors from the Literature

Research studies have found the following elements are part of an effective communication plan:

- Publicity about the benefits of change
- Publicity that highlights short-term successes

Biblical Corroboration in Nehemiah

When Nehemiah was ready to go public with his ideas, he called the leaders together and extolled the virtues of his vision and plan (2:16–18). They celebrated the short-term success of completing the wall with a great celebration (12:27–43).

An Example about Communication

At Willow Creek Church in Winter Springs, the weekly bulletin keeps a spotlight on men. Special-event announcements are regularly distributed to men. The church's website is also an active location for information on the men's discipleship program and activities.

When the men return from their annual May Wilderness Adventure, they have a dinner for all the men in the church about two weeks later. They show a brief highlights video (great to build interest for the next year) and give men three or four summer options to consider (e.g., a service project, a men's Sunday school class, a men's Bible study, and a social activity like paintball or mountain biking). Their philosophy is "don't surrender the summer."

WHAT YOU CAN DO | *To Promote Communication*

• Begin with a pervasive, organization-wide communication plan that reinforces your plans, and especially the vision for the program, at every opportunity. This includes bulletin items and inserts, pulpit announcements, and manned table displays in the foyer.

• Include personal invitations (actually, "repetitive" personal invitations). This is the most effective method of getting men involved.

• Mention your vision during sermons to increase perceived importance.

• Be sure the communication plan includes benefits of participation, and early success stories should be publicized. However, the leadership should be cautious about declaring victory too early.

THEME 8: RESISTANCE

Because of the fall, resistance is "built in." Paul said he would stay on at Ephesus, "because a great door for effective work has opened to me, *and there are many who oppose me*"(1 Corinthians 16:9, emphasis added).

You can expect resistance on two levels. First, there's *behavioral* resistance from individuals: people like routines, set patterns, and predictability; some feel threatened by meeting new people or programs that require time commitments. Second, there's *systemic* resistance from the church as an organization: a church operating at full tilt with no additional capacity will resist adding something else.

Implementation Factors from the Literature

Research studies have found the following elements are effective in dealing with resistance:

- Mechanisms to identify resistance
- Processes to deal with behavioral and systemic resistance

Biblical Corroboration in Nehemiah

Sanballat and Tobiah fiercely opposed Nehemiah and his plan, so the people "prayed to our God and posted a guard" (4:9). But that wasn't all—there were other types of internal resistance. The workers got tired, the rubble made it difficult to work (4:10), and others ran out of money (5:1–6). But Nehemiah had mechanisms to identify resistance (4:11–14). When they faced opposition, Nehemiah had worked out a communication plan to deal with resistance (4:19–20).

Examples of Resistance

Jim Smithies, pastor of lay ministries at Bethel Bible Church in Tyler, Texas, watched as his church resisted implementing the "Church of Irresistible Influence" model for reaching the community.[2] But through patience, time, and having a forum to process reservations, the church leaders eventually caught the vision. Pastor Smithies describes the process and eventual success:

> It took us a year to get the elders to consider trying to impact our community. We got to the point that there were two or three champions on the elder board that said, "This is a no-brainer. Biblically this is a no-brainer. We have a plan; we can't come up with any reason other than sinful self-centeredness for not trying this."
>
> So there is that persuasion phase, and eventually, if we're on a biblical path, the discipleship pathway, it's going to grow to the point where there are a couple champions on the elder board that say, "This is what we're going to do." Then my responsibility, and I think the senior pastor's responsibility, is to have a plan and people that can make it work. And, our climate is changing; it's easier now than it was. God has brought some new men on the elder board that want to become more purpose-driven and more outreach-driven and more discipleship-driven—so all of those components matter. It's very much an organism, and it's very much a dynamic. And I like that; you just have to be willing to deal with that in a relational context without ruining the relationships in the process of the frustration. And that's where, I think, it's been a challenge, and God has been merciful.

At Willow Creek Church, individual resistance from strong women who wish the senior pastor would devote more of his time to women's issues does come up from time to time. Pastor Pete Alwinson tried to win them over by saying something like, "In my opinion many of the issues in church and culture are caused by weak and immature men. I believe I can do more for women and children by equipping men to be stronger."

At Montgomery Community Church in Cincinnati, Pastor Tom Lipsey inherited and did not replace the church's senior leadership team. Those leaders wanted to cling to the old structure and strategy—ones that had failed to produce an effective church. Tom just waited. It took ten years, but most came around and those who didn't moved on.

WHAT YOU CAN DO | *To Respond to Resistance*

• Expect resistance. Don't presume your vision will just happen. Every substantial new idea will experience resistance, what we often call "pushback." And it is not just people who resist change (behavioral), but also the church as an organization (systemic) because the system will try to maintain the *status quo*. So it is important not to presume your vision will just happen, but actually to expect resistance.

• If considerable resistance is encountered, then program elements may need to be redesigned in response.

• Proactively identify resistance from both individuals and the church as a system trying to maintain equilibrium. The leaders and planners should discuss up front how they plan to process and deal with resistance. A strong communication plan, pilot programs, and allowing plenty of time for people to process the new idea may reduce or eliminate resistance.

• Keep talking about an idea until it either catches on or, through prayer, it becomes clear it is not God's will. Some of my smaller ideas catch on right away, but usually it takes many months and sometimes years for people to process the impact and implications of a substantial idea.

THEME 9: SUSTAINABILITY

Lots of really great, initially well-executed ideas bomb (remember the stats at the beginning of chapter 7). Sustaining the idea is the meat of the coconut.

By a wide margin, the reason pastors get so frustrated with pastoring men is the degree of difficulty they have sustaining ministries to men. After the initial flush of enthusiasm, "someone" has to keep men's discipleship ministry "center stage" until it becomes enfolded into the routines of the church.

The research reveals that "someone" is the pastor. The pastor is the key to everything—and that includes sustainability. It is your vision, your determination, your sustainable strategy that will make ministry to men last. Without your personal involvement, ministry to men probably won't happen. That's just reality.

How to sustain ministry to men needs to be part of the planning process from the beginning. In the next chapter I will show you how you can use the No Man Left Behind Model to build a sustainable strategy—one that will survive once the novelty wears off.

It will come as no surprise that the churches effective in men's discipleship knew how to sustain momentum, and the others did not. The word I think best describes the attitude of the pastors successful in reaching men is "determination." They just wouldn't take "no" for an answer. They were convinced they would ultimately prevail. They considered their efforts God's will. They were not to be denied.

Implementation Factor from the Literature

Research studies have found one key element that contributes to sustainability.

- Once the program is adopted, the leadership should enfold the initiative into the routines of the organization.

Biblical Corroboration in Nehemiah

Despite fierce resistance from within and without, Nehemiah and his team rebuilt the wall in fifty-two days. But the city was large, and the people were few (7:4). To sustain the vision and plans Nehemiah had started to implement, the city needed ongoing leadership. So Nehemiah appointed his brother to lead them (7:2). He appointed staff to maintain the city (7:3). And he repopulated Jerusalem with people (7:4–5). He repopulated the towns of Israel (7:73). He normalized Jerusalem and stabilized the land promised to his fathers.

An Example of Sustainability

Dennis McFadden, a pastor at Shoreline Community Church in Monterey, California, sustains momentum with men through their small groups. They found that a relationship-based, rather than an event-based, ministry model is more sustainable. They do events, but "events are just to give us an opening to create new relationships."

McFadden has worked men's discipleship into the routines of his church. Periodically McFadden appoints new leaders to the leadership team. Momentum is also sustained by letting men run with ministry ideas they come up with on their own. During Sunday service announcements McFadden will say something like, "Guys, did you like the last men's breakfast? What do you think?" And then the men who attended let out a roar. This builds equity in the event in the other men's eyes—a kind of tipping point. McFadden quotes Jesus, "'They'll know you're Christians by your love for one another.' We feel that's what's going to transform our church—the love our men have for one another. And we have to be in relationships for that to be manifested."

WHAT YOU CAN DO | *To Promote Sustainability*

• Help to sustain a new program by making it one of the habits, or routines, of your church. This is best accomplished if the initial planning considers how the program will be normalized in the church from the very start. "Routinization" is accomplished when people see how the church has truly benefited, staff have job descriptions that include men's discipleship support, and by insuring leadership successors are true believers in the program. Basically, sustainability is the by-product of putting the other eight of the nine themes in place.

• Stay focused on a huge goal for the long haul. There really are no shortcuts— whether business, ministry, or relationships. A shortcut takes years to develop. Often a small band of leaders stays the course. This group of leaders will often say things like: "We will prevail no matter what," and "We can do this." And they remind one another, "This is not going to be easy—nothing good is easy. But it will be worth it."

REMEMBER THE BIG THREE

We've looked at a host of success factors organized into nine essential themes. Frankly, that could get to be a bit overwhelming. But if you apply the three main factors discussed at the beginning of chapter 7, you will find the other factors will fall into line. Again, here are the big three:

- *Vision*: A vision to disciple *every* man in the church (the "all-inclusive" mindset).
- *Determination*: A personally involved pastor who is determined that men's discipleship will work "no matter what."
- *Sustainable Strategy*: A "sustainable" strategy to move men forward as disciples.

In the next chapter, I will offer a model you can use to build a sustainable strategy.

POINTS TO REMEMBER

Nine essential themes are present in every successful organization:
• Leadership
• Vision
• People
• Planning
• Resources
• Execution
• Communication plan
• Resistance
• Sustainability

REFERENCES FOR SUCCESS ACCESS

Books

Ansoff, Igor, and E. McDonnell. *Implanting Strategic Management.* 2nd ed. New York: Prentice Hall, 1990.

Collins, Jim. *Good to Great.* New York: HarperBusiness, 2001.

Kotter, John P. *Leading Change.* Boston: Harvard Business School, 1996.

Rogers, Everett M., and Everett Rogers. *Diffusion of Innovations.* 5th ed. New York: The Free Press, 2003.

Senge Peter M., Art Kleiner, Charlotte Roberts, and George Roth. *The Dance of Change.* New York: Doubleday, 1999.

Journals

Alexander, L. "Successfully Implementing Strategic Decisions." *Long Range Planning* 18, no. 3 (1985): 91–97.

Ayas, K., and N. Zeniuk. "Project-Based Learning: Building Communities of Reflective Practitioners." *Management Learning* 32, no. 1 (2001): 61–76.

Beer, M. "Why Total Quality Management Programs Do Not Persist." *Decision Sciences* 34, no. 4 (2003): 623–42.

Freedman, M. "The Genius Is in the Implementation." *Journal of Business Strategy* 24, no. 2 (2003): 26–31.

Houston-Philips, K. "Leadership Development Partnerships at Dow Corning Corporation." *Journal of Organizational Excellence* 22, no. 1 (2002): 13–27.

Johnson, K., C. Hays, H. Center, and C. Daley. "Building Capacity and Sustainable Prevention Innovations." *Evaluation and Program Planning* 27, no. 2 (2004): 135–49.

Kotter, J. P. "Leading Change: Why Transformation Efforts Fail." *Harvard Business Review* 73, no. 2 (1996): 59–67.

"Ten Observations." *Executive Excellence* (August 1999): 15–16.

"What Leaders Really Do." *Harvard Business Review* 79, no. 11 (2001): 85–96.

LeBrasseur, R., R. Whissell, and A. Ojha. "Organisational Learning, Transformational Leadership and Implementation of Continuous Quality Improvement in Canadian Hospitals." *Australian Journal of Management* 27, no. 2 (2002): 141–62.

Linton, J. D. "Implementation Research." *Technovation* 22, no. 2 (2002): 65–79.

Maurer, R. "Sustaining Commitment to Change." *The Journal for Quality & Participation* (Spring 2005): 30–35.

McNish, M. "Guidelines for Managing Change." *Journal of Change Management* 2, no. 3 (2002): 201–11.

Miller, D. "Successful Change Leaders." *Journal of Change Management* 2, no. 4 (2002): 359–68.

Okumus, F. "A Framework to Implement Strategies in Organizations." *Management Decision* 41 (9) (2003): 871–82.

Pluye, P., L. Potvin, and J. Denis. "Making Public Health Programs Last." *Evaluation & Program Planning* 27, no. 2 (2004): 121–33.

Popper, M., and R. Lipshitz. "Installing Mechanisms and Instilling Values: The Role of Leaders in Organizational Learning." *The Learning Organization* 7, no. 3 (2000): 134–44.

Repenning, N. P. "A Simulation-Based Approach to Understanding the Dynamics of Innovation Implementation." *Organization Science: A Journal of the Institute of Management Sciences* 13, no. 2 (2002): 109–27.

Thurston, P. H. "Should Smaller Companies Make Formal Plans?" *Harvard Business Review* 61, no. 5 (1983):162–88.

THE NO MAN LEFT BEHIND MODEL: A SUSTAINABLE STRATEGY TO DISCIPLE EVERY WILLING MAN IN YOUR CHURCH

Easily the number one issue with ministry to men is *sustainability*: how do you keep it going? You've no doubt tried to have a "men's ministry." It was probably easy to start, perhaps built around a specific curriculum or a charismatic leader—two of the "easiest" ways to get something going without a comprehensive plan. But it no doubt petered out just as easily—the proverbial roller-coaster experience.

Here's the real problem. Every time "men's ministry" fails, it's like a little inoculation. So the next time a lay leader wants to build a men's ministry, you're a little reluctant. You've been burned. But because he's such an influential layman, you give him the green light. And then it fails again. Perhaps the leader's work hours changed, maybe he moved away, or he may have thought he could just get it going and then dump it in your lap. Whatever the reason, it's another failed attempt. And another inoculation.

After three or four such failed attempts, the church's resistance is complete and impenetrable. Men's ministry gets the reputation of being "a loser." You become convinced, *Men's ministry just won't work here.*

I would like to make a promise. You can defeat this start-stop, roller-coaster syndrome by adopting a whole new way of thinking about reaching men. I'm about to show you a carrot so big that I hope, no matter how badly you've been burned in the past, you'll want to give it a try.

That carrot is the No Man Left Behind Model—a simple yet robust model you can adopt to build an *intentional, sustainable* men's discipleship ministry to *all* of your men. Based on the book *No Man Left Behind*, coauthored with David Delk and Brett Clemmer, the No Man Left Behind Model has been under the microscope of continuous improvement since 1996.

In the previous two chapters, we looked at the multiple success factors necessary to effectively implement men's discipleship—or, for that matter, any major initiative. I also highlighted the three main research-based factors for effective men's discipleship: a *vision* to disciple every man, the *determination* to make it happen, and a *sustainable strategy* to keep it going.

If you have read this far, you no doubt already have the vision and the determination to pastor your men. The final, and hardest, piece of the puzzle is to put the right strategy in motion—one that will still be working ten years from now. This is the point where "models" come into play. If a strategy includes "everything that needs to be done to succeed," then models conflate that "everything" into a simple—and hence manageable—process. Having the right model is essential. As one scholar said,

> One key reason why implementation fails is that practicing executives, managers and supervisors do not have practical, yet theoretically sound, models to guide their actions during implementation. Without adequate models, they try to implement strategies without a good understanding of the multiple factors that must be addressed, often simultaneously, to make implementation work.[1]

In business there's an axiom, "Your system is perfectly designed to produce the results you are getting." This model, depicted in figure 2, is a system perfectly designed to help you call, equip, and send every willing man in your church to become a passionate follower of Christ at each man's own pace.

The model is simple. You can sketch it on a paper napkin at breakfast with one of your leaders. The vision is to help men grow as disciples and disciple-makers. On the left you have men who need Christ. A conveyor belt moves "every man" along toward discipleship and spiritual maturity at his own pace.

The create-capture-sustain cycle is the engine that powers the conveyor belt. Multiple repetitions of the create-capture-sustain cycle keep the conveyor belt moving. The conveyor belt is built on three foundations. And the model works best when the church in general has *a disciple-making culture.*

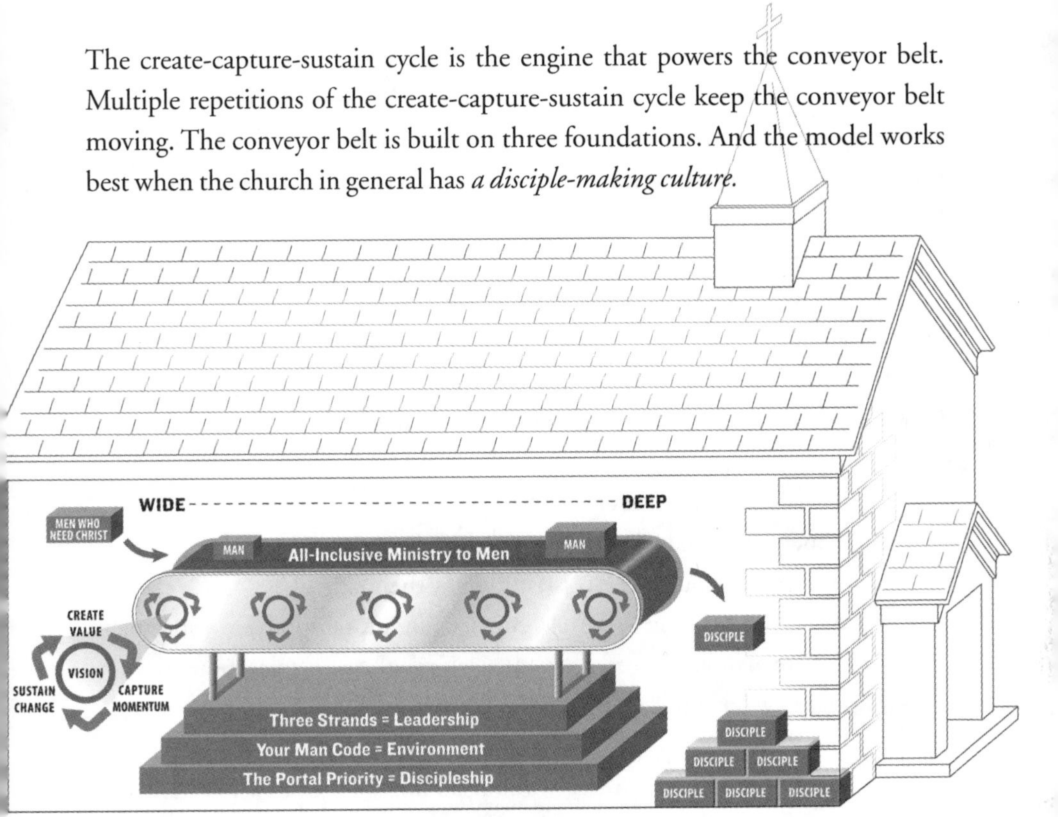

FIGURE 2
The No Man Left Behind Model

No Man Left Behind is *not* something you "add" to your already busy schedule. It's *not* an additional "program." It's *not* a "curriculum."

Rather, it's a *process*—an "intentional" process to help you create an environment where the Holy Spirit inspires men to engage in life-on-life discipleship. You overlay it on top of your existing ministry. It will give you and your leaders a common language to organize what you are *already* doing to maximize your disciple-making impact. And it will reveal new areas of opportunity to disciple your men—*all* of them.

When our field staff consult with churches, these are the concepts from which they draw. Thousands of churches and leaders have been trained and are using No Man Left Behind. For example, Grace Community Church in Indianapolis, a church of 7,000 with 2,500 men, wanted to more effectively disciple men. After a couple of false starts, several of the lay leaders had dramatically different ideas about which way to go (in short, what the "model" should be).

So they sent a caravan of fifteen men to attend a No Man Left Behind Conference in Cincinnati. In the seven years since, in the words of Mike Whitesell, the men's pastor, they have "increased in numbers from dozens gathering regularly to hundreds. There are presently hundreds of men discipling other men who have already agreed to begin doing the same within a year."

Whether you have 25 men, 250 men, or 2,500 men, you also can "[produce] a crop, yielding a hundred, sixty, or thirty times what was sown" (Matthew 13:23) using the No Man Left Behind Model. By the end of this chapter you will understand how to more effectively do the following:

- Attract new men to your church
- Help men who need Christ come to faith
- Help lukewarm Cultural Christians renew their faith
- Give new believers and Cultural Christians an "on-ramp" to grow spiritually
- Assimilate men into your *existing* or *new* growth and service ministries
- Surface new servant leaders and disciple-makers for your church

And you will be able to do this without adding a lot of new programming or work for yourself. Sound too good to be true? Let's dig in so you can see for yourself.

Here are fifteen concepts to make sure no willing man in your church gets left behind.

AN "ALL-INCLUSIVE" MINDSET

My colleagues and I have spent more than twenty-five years studying why and how some churches disciple men effectively while others languish or fail. Of all the insights we've gained, none is more important than this: *Successful churches have a vision to disciple all their men, not just those willing to join "men's only" activities.* We call this the "all-inclusive" mindset.

The "old wineskin" men's ministry model was a small group of six men meeting for Bible study at zero dark thirty on Wednesday mornings and twelve guys eating burned pancakes together once a month on a Saturday morning. In the old way of thinking, if you had that much going, you had men's ministry covered. You could check that box.

But what about the men who are part of the worship team, teach middle school boys, park cars, usher, only attend the weekly worship service, or just show up for holidays? How do they become strong disciples?

Where did we ever get the idea that any more than a small fraction of men would be interested in joining a "men's only" ministry? The activities of the "old wineskin" were inherently designed to attract only the most dedicated men. Perfectly executed, that model might involve 25 percent of your men, tops.[2] The more you think about it, the more the old way of reaching men sounds like a design flaw on par with the Hindenburg—a small gondola strapped to a highly flammable balloon. It was doomed from the start.

For these reasons, we believe the term "men's ministry" is a spoiled term, in some places even toxic.

When we consult with churches, one of the first questions we ask is, "Where are men already growing and serving in your church?" Most churches are shocked—literally—at all the good things already going on with their men. But they didn't see it that way because it wasn't being done in the men's only "silos" typically thought of as men's ministry.

So broaden your thinking. Any activity or event where men are involved is another lane to help you reach men. For example, the graduation ceremony for vacation Bible school, couples' home groups, a tour of the local food bank, the annual fall festival, or the annual Easter egg hunt that draws families from the community to the church grounds.

So what's the "new wineskin" for reaching men? Simply, *however many men you have in your church, that's the size of your ministry to men.* In the example above, six men are in a Bible study and twelve attend a monthly fellowship breakfast. Let's say this is in a church of 100 men. So what is the size of the men's ministry? In the old way of thinking, the answer would have been eighteen men. But in the "all-inclusive" mindset, the answer is 100 men.

Building an "all-inclusive disciple-making ministry to our men" is the "new wineskin" for reaching men.

In fact, we suggest you even stop using the term "men's ministry" altogether—it can help you shed the baggage of the old way that reaches only some of your men.

So help your leaders see that everything your church does that touches men is "ministry to men," from the worship service to ushering to kitchen helper. An "all-inclusive ministry to men" disciples men right where they are. For example, you don't need your male Sunday school teachers—men already doing what disciples do—to join a separate ministry to men. Instead, have them gather thirty minutes early once a month to build camaraderie and to discuss "the challenges of being a male Sunday school teacher."

Why is the "all-inclusive" mindset so important? The mission is "Go and make disciples." Jesus said it in the form of a command, which makes it a moral imperative. And experience shows why. Anything less than a plan to disciple every *willing* man will become, for all concerned, a moral failure of catastrophic proportion. Of course, we are not responsible for how our men respond, but we *are* responsible that *all* of them hear the call in a compelling way.

But here's the rub. Not all men are the same.

FIVE TYPES OF MEN:
WHY "ONE SIZE FITS ALL" DOESN'T WORK

Early in our research it became clear that many leaders were using a "one size fits all" approach to reach their men. But as every car manufacturer knows, they can't offer only one model in one color and expect much success. That only worked in the very early days of the industry. In the same way, "one size fits all" ministry to men may have worked fifty years ago, but those days are long gone.

Here's an example of how once size fits all plays out today. David Delk, our President and Co-CEO, who has been at this full-time since 1994, tells about the time his church put on a men's weekend retreat with speakers on topics like marriage and family with lots of recreation and free time sprinkled in. Eighty men attended the event, including fourteen men on the fringe of the church who might not ordinarily attend. Several men received Jesus or renewed their faith, eleven of those fourteen men signed up for six-week follow-up groups, and many new relationships were formed with the potential for ongoing impact.

David and several other leaders were so excited and pleased. However, during the leadership team debrief, some of the men expressed deep disappointment about the weekend. David was shocked. One man, whose passion is developing deep relationships, thought that they should have formed groups of four men for the weekend, and after each speaker, they should have sent the men back to their cabins for discussion, ending in a time of group prayer. Another man thought they should have had more time for worship, since the men went to all the trouble to get away at the event. Another man thought they should not have had as much free time, but perhaps provided some personal Bible study and devotional material to go along with the messages.

What happened, of course, was that different leaders had different ministry callings and passions to impact different types of men. We all have our favorites, don't we? Once a group of leaders understand this propensity, everyone can relax, celebrate God's different gifts and callings, and know they'll be able to plan ministries that reach their favorite "size" on another occasion.

Since you want to be "all-inclusive" and "intentional," you're going to need more than one "size." There's no one right way to do this, but every man is on a spiritual journey. Taking a cue from that idea, in the field we find five types of men at various stages on their journeys. These five "sizes" of men fit along what we call "the wide-deep continuum," illustrated here.

THE FIVE TYPES OF MEN

Need Christ **ME**	Cultural Christians **ME & GOD**	Biblical Christians **GOD & ME**	Servant Leaders **GOD & OTHERS**

WIDE — — — — — — — — — — — **DEEP**

← Hurting Men →

On the wide side, to the far left, are **Men Who Need Christ.** Next are **Cultural Christians**, the men who lead lukewarm lives. Then **Biblical Christians**, men who are disciples, or want to be. And on the deep side of the continuum, to the far right, are **Servant Leaders**, men who are disciple-makers and candidates for leadership roles in the church, such as leading growth groups, leading a serve team, deacon, or elder.

Hurting Men, those with "broken wings," span across the whole spectrum of the other four types. It's likely that 50–70 percent of your men are going through a major marriage, children, work, money, or health crisis, self-destructive behavior, loss of meaning, or other crisis at a given time—without respect to spiritual maturity.

You can immediately see the value of knowing to which group a man belongs. Obviously, a man well versed in the Bible with a gift for leadership and administration has different needs than an unsaved man or a nominal Christian whose wife has just issued an ultimatum to get straight or get out.

As noted above, you probably feel especially drawn to one of these five types of men. Maybe it's evangelizing lost men. Maybe it's working with homeless men. Possibly it's getting men into small groups. Perhaps you prefer mobilizing men who are already strong Christians. Here's the point: unless you have an *intentional* process to reach all five types of men, you may end up stunting the growth and ministry of your men and, as a result, your whole church. One size fits all just doesn't work. Appendix C includes actual examples of how Pastor Jeff Kisiah engaged all five types of men at Harvest Community Church in Charlotte, North Carolina, and a worksheet for you to think through what you are already doing and could add to reach each type of man.

Now let's look at how No Man Left Behind actually works in practice.

THE CREATE-CAPTURE-SUSTAIN CYCLE

Let's start with the engine: the create-capture-sustain cycle. We've all watched a football game where one team seemed to have the game sewed up. But they made a couple of mistakes, the other team got excited, made a big play and, suddenly, the momentum was gone. The heart of the No Man Left Behind Model is managing momentum by "creating value, capturing momentum, and sustaining change." Figure 3 illustrates the create-capture-sustain cycle.[3]

FIGURE 3
The Create-Capture-Sustain Cycle

CLARIFY YOUR VISION

First, notice that everything revolves "around" vision. Men want to be part of something bigger than themselves. Except for those dependable few men who will do whatever you ask, most men won't attend an activity or get involved with a ministry unless they feel like it's going somewhere, especially younger men.

In one way or another, the essence of your vision is "to disciple every man in the church." The endgame is to call, equip, and send men to become passionate followers of Jesus Christ. "We disciple men"—this is how you talk about the vision with your leaders.

Make sure your leaders are on the same page up front. A split or unclear vision will create a lot of discord down the road. Repeat your vision whenever you get together with your men's discipleship leaders, whether formally or over coffee.

Visions are more powerful than labor. A compelling vision will set forces in motion that, once released, can no longer be contained.

A PUBLIC SLOGAN

You will also want a "public" vision statement—a "slogan"—that resonates with your men. Find a sentence or phrase that inspires your men, like "no man left behind." Or my favorite, "to help men grow as disciples and disciple-makers— starting at home."

Keep it short—they'll remember. Keep it concrete—they'll visualize what you mean. Keep it pithy—they'll repeat it. Keep it noble—it will give them a sense of destiny and purpose. Touch their felt needs—they'll get involved.

AN ALL-INCLUSIVE NAME

In addition to clarifying the vision for the leadership team and adopting a slogan for your "public" vision statement, you will also want to come up with an "all-inclusive name"—one that unmistakably applies to *all* your men. For example, Men of Grace (as at Mike Whitesell's Grace Community Church). Or perhaps Kingdom Men, Men of Valor, or Iron Men.

Don't *ever* make men feel like they have to be part of your "men's only" ministry to be part of the "Men of Grace." Instead, describe *any* and *every* involvement men have with your church as something that the "Men of Grace" are doing.

The men who serve as deacons, the men who lead the scout troop, the men who play in the worship band, and the men who teach the fifth graders—none of those men would be included in the old definition of "men's ministry" as separate men's programming. But all of them are vital to the vision God has for your church for "no man left behind" (or whatever you decide). So thank them for being "Men of Grace" (or whatever name you choose).

A COMMON LANGUAGE

Since the term "disciple" can mean different things to different people, you will want to create a common language.

Plan to preach a series on discipleship—something like, "What Is a Disciple, and How Do You Become One?" Focus on the biblical command to make disciples, texts that describe discipleship (see figure 1, chapter 5), examples of how Jesus' disciples responded, and examples of discipleship—calling, equipping, and sending—that are already taking place in your church.

For example, tell them about Michael, who never before did much of anything but became excited about serving Christ through Meals on Wheels and, as a result, recently signed up for a growth group. I'll say more on this in a few pages under the subheading "Create a Disciple-Making Culture."

For illustration purposes, let's say you have adopted the public vision statement "every man a disciple and disciple-maker—starting at home." It's clear what you mean, pithy, memorable, biblical, and bold. Here's an example of how the create-capture-sustain cycle "revolves" around the vision.

CREATE VALUE

Every time you ask a man to do something, he consciously or subconsciously compares it to other possible uses of his time. In essence, he's looking at the "value proposition" of what you're offering. You can create momentum by offering men something they want—"something of value." That may be inviting them to have breakfast, attend church, play softball, take a mission trip to Haiti, or be your guest at a special men's event.

Suppose you plan and execute a very successful event or activity that includes men. It could be a "men only" event like a fireside chat with the pastor on a Sunday night, a wild beast feast, a fall bonfire, a season of softball, a seminar on a men's issue, or something as simple as inviting a hurting man to have a cup of coffee. Or it could be a strong man competition at the annual Fall Festival, a daddy-daughter dance, or taking sandwiches and blankets to homeless people.

Presently, let's say five of your 100 men are passionate about men's discipleship and are, in their own right, strong disciple-makers. You may have more, but let's go with five. Let's say you ask, and they accept the challenge, to plan and execute a men's dinner with an outside speaker on the topic "Success That Matters." Collectively, they invest a whopping one hundred hours to push the event over the top. The marketing resonates with your men. They perceive the event will be a "valuable" use of their limited time. Forty of your 100 men attend. It's the single best men's event you've ever had. You're jazzed.

Now what? Danger alert: this is precisely the point at which most ministry to men stalls. A golden key to sustain what you start is the concept of "capturing momentum."

CAPTURE MOMENTUM

Every church, pastor, and men's leadership team wants to know how to get more "stick" out of their events, worship services, and activities.

Here's the heartburn. It is so disappointing to expend all that energy to turn men out, then see them drift away when the event is over. Unless you pre-planned something to capture the momentum, you may as well heat your home to a comfortable 72 degrees in the dead of winter and then leave your windows and the front door open. You've expended a lot of energy, but have not captured it. This, as much as any other error, is what makes for a roller-coaster ministry to men.

Frankly, it just takes too much effort not to have a fabulously desirable "next right step" to suggest for each man. It might be as simple as inviting a man to church or to meet (or meet again) for coffee. It might be a six-week study on a topical issue he's interested in, such as marriage, parenting, or how to be a leader. Anything. Just don't let him slip away! Obviously, some men are not ready for a next step, but what about those who are? Not to offer that step is, in some sense, failing that man's discipleship.

Instead, offer what we call a "believable next right step" for the men who attend the "Success That Matters" dinner (or other event)—a step to help "capture" the momentum. First and foremost, be a "closer." Suggest, then close, on the next right step before you adjourn.

Imagine walking into an automobile showroom and spotting the car you've always wanted—a shiny red convertible. You walk around the car several times leaving drool as you go. A salesperson walks up and says, "She sure is a beauty, isn't she?" You respond with how much you love this car!

What would you think if the salesperson said, "I can see you really want this car. I tell you what. Why don't you give me your name and phone number, and I will give you a call in a couple of weeks to see if you're still interested?"

The last thing you want to do is collect names and tell men you'll get back to them. Two weeks later, after you've sorted the cards by zip codes, most men will have forgotten they even checked the box! Yet that's exactly what happens when churches expend a lot of energy and resources to turn men out, but then don't help them identify their next step right there on the spot.

Also, be sure to avoid the opposite error. Don't ask a man for too big of a commitment—such as a three-year commitment to an inductive Bible study in the original Greek starting with a forty-day fast as a way to wrap up a season on your church softball team. That guy is more likely the man you invite to church or for that cup of coffee.

The greatest amount of energy required in nature is that amount necessary to overcome inertia. It takes a lot of energy and creativity to get a man moving. So don't throw it away. Once you get a man in motion, capture the momentum. And do it on the spot. It's the discipleship thing to do.

Okay, now back to your "Success That Matters" event. How do you take the next right step? You could, for example, say, "Men, we've had a wonderful time tonight hearing about God's perspective on success. For the next six weeks we're going to have discussion groups meet for one hour a week to unpack more about success that matters."

You have already purchased follow-up booklets with six weeks of discussion questions. You put them in the middle of the table—enough for every man. You form the men into groups of five or six right there on the spot, while the iron is hot.

Happily, twenty-seven of the forty men sign up. You tell them to pick a leader, a mutually convenient meeting time and place, write down everyone's names and contact information, and set their first meeting.

Our records show that after conducting way north of one thousand events, an average of two-thirds of your men will take the offer and join a short-term follow-up group. That's because it is a "second gear" task. In other words, instead of trying to shift them from "first gear" (the event) to "fourth gear" (a long-term Bible study or taking a missions trip), you give them a believable next step. The men hear your offer and think, "I can do that." They can visualize themselves succeeding at what you've suggested, which is huge.

SUSTAIN CHANGE

How do you sustain the spiritual change and transformation once it's under way? What do you do with the men once the six-week groups are over? Well before the groups end—at weeks four and five—you begin to plant seeds for the next right "sustain" steps. From the pulpit, you mention the discussion groups. Have a man give a testimony about how God is using the group to change his life. Then you give your men several options.

The concept is to assimilate men into the "existing" growth and service ministries of the church. You can also offer something "new." This is the silver bullet—the way you can use the No Man Left Behind Model to populate the new and existing growth and service ministries of your church. You can also use these groups to identify men with leadership potential for further elder or deacon training.

Remember, men do what *they* want—not what *you* want. So offer several options for both growth ("equipping") and service ("sending"). In theory, you could offer equipping and sending opportunities for each of the five types of men—a total of ten options. In practice, offer a manageable handful appropriate for the men you targeted with your "create value" step. Here are some examples.

- A book study that will discuss a chapter a week (Types 1, 2, 3, 4)
- Becoming part of a recovery group (Types 1, 5)
- An opportunity to visit one of three local ministries to the poor and homeless (Types 1–5)
- Joining an existing Bible study or home group (Types 2, 3, 4, 5)
- Joining the prison ministry team on its next trip (Types 2, 3, 4, 5)
- Starting a new Bible study or home group (Types 3, 4)
- Any ministry of the church that needs volunteers (Types 3, 4)
- Becoming part of the Men's Leadership Team (Types 3, 4)
- A class to uncover his spiritual gifts (Type 3)
- A "how to find your service niche in the church" meeting during the Sunday school hour (Types 3, 4)
- A missions trip (Type 4, 5)
- Leadership training for elders or deacons (Type 4)
- An ongoing weekly discipleship Bible study that you teach as pastor (Types 3, 4, 5)

Later, you can repeat the create-capture-sustain cycle with something that targets a different type(s) of men.

Also, keep in mind two special groups of men. Some of the men in your six-week groups may already be up to their eyebrows in growth and service, so they will go back to what they were doing. Give disciples like them a nod as you speak. It is discouraging to be all out for Christ and never get a word of appreciation and encouragement. Or worse, to feel like you've been spanked for not taking on more.

Another group of your men may need to rest, not hear about more to do. Give men in your church permission to "come to me all you who are weary and burdened" and take a season to rest. Let them be "takers" until they are filled to the overflow in their relationship with Jesus and *want* to become "givers." The key word here is "want." Yes, you can get men to do what they "need" to do for a while, but ultimately men will always end up doing what they "want." So let them worship, hear about Christ's love, abide in Him, and, at a point, they will naturally *want* to do something to better know and serve their Lord from a heart you gave the grace and space to fill up with gratitude.

How many men can you expect to be involved after one cycle of create-capture-sustain?

RESISTANCE: THE PRINCIPLE OF
THE PARABLE OF THE SOWER

The command to make disciples must always be juxtaposed against the principle of the parable of the sower. Jesus said, "Go and make disciples." He also said that when we do, some seed will fall on the path and be snatched, some will fall on rocky soil and will spring up but soon wither, some will be choked by life's worries and riches, but some *will* produce a crop.

Remember, overcoming resistance is one of the nine major themes of successfully implementing organizational change. The resistance here is the inertia in men. Because of the principle of the parable of the sower, attrition is "expected" every time you ask for additional involvement.

So what is a reasonable set of expectations for a pastor of a hundred men who has forty of them attend an event?

TAKING STOCK: SUCCESS OR FAILURE?

In our example, forty men came to the "create value" event and 67 percent— twenty-seven men—joined the six-week "capture momentum" follow-up groups. Let's suppose that once those groups run their course, out of the twenty-seven men, five take up your offer for more "equipping" and/or "sending." I know that sounds low, and you may get more. But let's stick with five men for our illustration.

Think about it. You have a hundred men in your church. You turned forty of them out for a great event that in and of itself accomplished quite a bit of discipleship. The speaker's message hit several key points about stewardship of money (equipping). The speaker's evangelistic close resulted in one man becoming a Christian, and six men rededicating their lives (calling). Then thirty-four of those men went through a six-week group. That's quite a bit more discipleship (equipping). And now you have five new men previously inactive who are involved in the life of the church at a whole new level (equipping and sending). And their families will become more involved too.

If you had not "captured" and "sustained" the momentum, the man who professed faith and the six men who rededicated would likely have slipped through the cracks. The lessons learned about money from the speaker would have been like seed scattered on rocky soil. Maybe one man might have on his own initiative figured out how to get more involved. Instead, you laid down "tracks" for the men to run on and allowed for the following:

- One man received Christ
- Six men renewed their faith
- Twenty-seven men dug deeper into success that matters
- Five new men got involved in ongoing discipleship (equipping and sending)

Let's say that before your event, 25 percent of your 100 men were already disciples. That's twenty-five men. You just added five more, for a 20 percent increase in the number of men committed to discipleship. And all that happened in just a single ninety-day cycle of create-capture-sustain—including the planning time. Impressive. Any businessman would jump at an opportunity for that kind of return on investment.

Here's what one cycle of the No Man Left Behind Model looks like. Note how it accounts for men dropping away because of the principle of the parable of the sower:

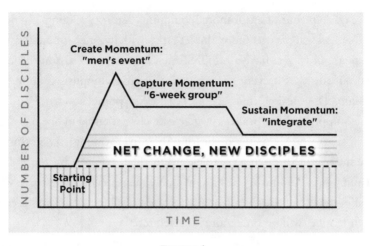

FIGURE 4
One Repetition of the Create-Capture-Sustain Cycle

What would have happened if you did not have a strategy to capture and sustain momentum from your event? After a few weeks you would be right back where you started—as though the event had never happened. It would only have registered as a "blip." So the "net change, new disciples" may not seem like much at first, but it's a lot compared to the alternative of doing nothing.

REPEAT THE CREATE-CAPTURE-SUSTAIN CYCLE: THE CONVEYOR BELT

So you've completed one cycle. Now what? This is where it starts to get interesting. This is where sustainable long-term growth and change becomes a real possibility for your church.

Once a cycle has run its course, you repeat the cycle. I like to think of this as "steady plodding." It's like a people mover that steadily moves men forward.

Repetition builds on the momentum already in place—like the flywheel concept in Jim Collins's *Good to Great*. Every revolution of the create-capture-sustain cycle allows for incremental progress by taking small steps forward. Without a repeating cycle, it seems unlikely that an effective ongoing program could be implemented. The conveyor belt in our model would simply stop moving.

Here's what three cycles of create-capture-sustain look like:

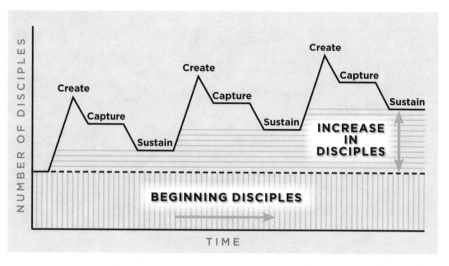

FIGURE 5
Three Repetitions of the Create-Capture-Sustain Cycle

This model is thrilling because it's believable, manageable, doable, and—best of all—it works. This approach pulsates to the rhythm of the gospels. Many repetitions will help work the create-capture-sustain cycle into the "routines" of the church—in essence, a sustainable strategy. That's what leads to the 48 percent increase in male attendance and 84 percent increase in male discipleship mentioned in chapter 1.

And there you have it—a "system perfectly designed to disciple men into passionate followers of Jesus Christ."

Now let's turn our attention to the foundations upon which the model is built—the "portal priority" (your philosophy of ministry), a "man code" (the environment you create for men), and the "three strands of leadership."

THE PORTAL PRIORITY

Suppose a man has attended your church for four months. What will he think is the first priority—the organizing idea—of your church?

One week he hears that worship ought to be a top priority. The next week he hears that he needs to be a cheerful giver. The following week he hears that committed believers go on mission trips. The week after that he is asked to attend evangelism training. The next week he learns about the compelling needs at the crisis pregnancy center. A weekend seminar greatly emphasizes the importance of private study and devotions. If you were a new man in Christ, what would you think? Unfortunately, this can be very confusing to the average man in the pew. It can look like an undifferentiated blob of disconnected activities as shown in figure 6.

	Preaching	Teaching	Christian Literature		
Leadership Training	Godly Families	Service/ Missions		Worship	Bible Studies
	Fellowship	Discipleship	Evangelism		
Informal Discussions	Stewardship	Social Justice Ministry		Vocation	Private Study
	Seminars	Mentoring	Small Groups		

FIGURE 6
Undifferentiated Church Priorities and Activities
(as they appear to a relative newcomer)

With so many priorities, is it any wonder some men end up confused? The sheer number of priorities seems overwhelming! What's the starting point? Where does he focus? Where do *you* focus? Consider a few more questions:

- How can a man worship a God he does not know?
- How can a man have genuine fellowship unless he knows why he should love his neighbor as himself?
- How can a man be a good steward if he doesn't understand and believe that everything he has is a gift from God—his time, talent, and his treasures?
- How can a man serve effectively if he doesn't know his gifts and that God can use him—or even that God wants to use him?
- How can a man perform acts of mercy if he doesn't know that he's to love the poor?
- Why would a man want to share his faith if he doesn't understand the Great Commission?

As you can see in figure 7, one idea sits squarely in the center of all the other *desired outcomes*. The focusing priority of a thriving church is discipleship. Sheep cannot do right until they know right.

Discipleship is the "portal" priority through which all the other priorities of your church can be achieved. It is the method of Jesus (Matthew 28:18–20) and the first of the three foundations in figure 2. Organize your church by putting discipleship in the center, and then draw arrows out to each of your desired outcomes (yours may vary) like this:

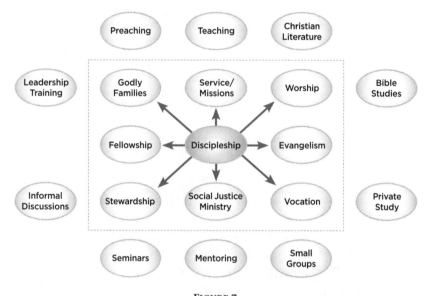

FIGURE 7
Desired Church Outcomes
Organized around Discipleship as the "Portal" Priority

Next, how can your church implement discipleship as the portal priority? The items around the outside of figures 6 and 7 represent the *methods* a church engages in to help build disciples. Now let's draw arrows from each method to the portal priority (see figure 8). Remember, these methods are not ends in themselves, but the means by which we help people learn and live out what it means to be a disciple. All the methods on the outside lead to discipleship in the middle, producing the desired outcomes.

Now we have a clear picture of discipleship as the portal priority by which every other goal of the church can be accomplished. For example, we don't preach to make "worshipers" but to make "disciples" who see God in a way that men can't help but worship. We don't preach to make "workers" but to make "disciples" who understand that bearing much fruit brings glory to God (John 15:8).

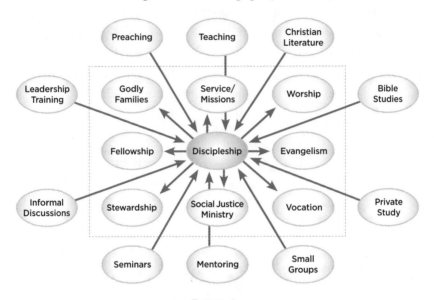

FIGURE 8
Methods of Making Disciples to Reach Other
Church Priorities and Goals

The focus is not, for example, "feed the poor." It's "make disciples," some of whom, as a result, catch a vision for feeding the poor.

To reiterate, discipleship is the portal priority through which all the other priorities of a church can be achieved. The portal priority concept can give you and your leaders a way to filter your activities and programs to keep a tighter focus on your vision.

While we're on the portal priority, let's take a short detour. Let's pause from talking about men's discipleship for a moment, and talk about discipleship in general.

CREATE A DISCIPLE-MAKING CULTURE

We can talk about the importance of men's discipleship until we are blue in the face, but there's something that a church must have in place before men's discipleship can get any real traction: a disciple-making culture.

We see this with striking clarity in the field: churches with great momentum because they already have a disciple-making culture, compared to churches that even with great men's leaders can't keep the momentum because the church in general does not have a disciple-making culture that supports their work.

One leader asked, "Since many/most churches would say they *are* creating such a culture, what would you define as the tangible characteristics of a church that truly is creating a disciple-making culture?"

It's a good point and a great question. How can you create a disciple-making culture? The starting point to creating a disciple-making culture is by implementing the answers to three simple questions: *What is a disciple? What is discipleship? And what is a disciple-maker?*

First, create a clear understanding about the "end product" you're trying to produce. In other words, what *is* a disciple? A disciple is someone "called" to live *in* Christ (salvation, abide), "equipped" to live *like* Christ (spiritual formation and growth), and "sent" to live *for* Christ (neighbor love, bear fruit).

These three tangible results will be happening all the time in a disciple-making culture: men (and women and children) will regularly be coming to Jesus by faith (calling), growing in their faith (equipping), and serving the Lord through love and deeds (sending). We like this three-part definition because it is both *biblical* and *actionable*. In other words, you can build ministry initiatives around it, and you can measure progress.

Second, create a clear picture of the "process" by which disciples are made. In other words, what is discipleship? Discipleship is not a "program," although discipleship curricula can be part of the process. Here's a better way to think of it—a more organic way, similar to the process Jesus used. *When God puts someone in your path who is stuck, discipleship means finding out why and then helping them solve that problem.*

What are those problems? Here are the seven top reasons, from my book *Man Alive,* that men will feel they are stuck: "I feel like I am in this alone, I don't feel like God cares about me personally, my life has no purpose, I have destructive behaviors that keep dragging me down, my soul feels dry, my most important relationships are not healthy, and I don't feel like I'm doing anything that will leave the world a better place." When a man walks into your church, it's usually for one or more of these seven reasons.

Third, create a disciple-making culture by raising up many "disciple-makers." What do these disciple-makers look like? Let's say a man walks through the front door of your church for the very first time with his wife and children. Imagine squads of men trained to mobilize and take action—men who have sat around a table and wrestled with the questions, "Why did he just do that? Why would a man visit our church? What is the problem he is trying to solve?" They understand what a big step it is for a man to walk through your door.

Those men are your disciple-makers. Disciple-makers are the ones who will take other men under their wings and show them the ropes—the spiritually mature men who will show the new guys how to become godly men, husbands, and fathers. They care, because someone once cared about them.

So how are you doing? Here are three questions that can help you assess the degree to which your church has a disciple-making culture:

- *Disciples*: Are we regularly calling, equipping, and sending people?
- *Discipleship*: When God brings us people who are stuck, do we have a process to find out why, and then help them solve their problems?
- *Disciple-Makers*: Do we have men (and women) who are intentionally making disciples who will, in turn, disciple others?

Concentrate on implementing good answers to these three questions, and you will increasingly create a disciple-making culture.

Now that we have established the portal priority of "discipleship" as the first foundation, let's look at the second foundation.

YOUR MAN CODE

How do men dress at your church—casual clothes, slacks and sports coat, business casual? When a new man starts attending, how many weeks do you think it will take him to figure out what to wear? You obviously don't publish a dress code, but every man still figures out the dress code in about one week, right?

In the same way, you have an unwritten "man code" that defines what it means to be a man in your church. The man code is the second foundation shown in figure 2. Like the dress code, your men observe what is expected of them to be a man in your church. And being performance-oriented, men will tend to give you back exactly what you ask for. If you want them to be strong disciples—spiritual leaders, men of integrity, and strong husbands and fathers—then they will work to those ends.

When we train groups of church leadership teams, we have them do an exercise. First, each team comes up with their church's *existing* man code and shares it with the larger group. Some are on target, some get a laugh, and some are downright sad. One pastor said the existing man code was, "Successful men welcome." Another, "Men are tolerated." Another leader said the vibe they gave off to men was, "If you think you're tired now, join our church, and we'll show you what tired really means!" Obviously they all were eager to make a change.

After round one, we have them come up with what they *want* their man code to be going forward. Examples include,

- "Men are important here."
- "This church values men."
- "Men are godly husbands and fathers."
- "Men are pursuing Christ."
- "Men are building God's kingdom."

From the décor, to the announcements, to how men are involved in the worship service, you can create an atmosphere that says: "Men matter here. Men can make a difference. God is doing something in and through the men of this church." Would you need to modify your "man code" for men to feel like this?

THE THREE STRANDS OF LEADERSHIP

Successful discipleship ministries for men need strong support from the senior pastor, a committed leader, and an effective leadership team—three strands of leadership (like the cord of three strands in Ecclesiastes 4:12). These form the third foundation in figure 2.

We've already detailed your involvement as the pastor. You certainly don't have to attend every meeting, but you do need to regularly ask the questions, "Are my men being discipled?" and "How can I help?"

You also need a passionate leader who wakes up in the morning praying that God would use him to help disciple the men of your church and community. Don't let this leader self-select himself into the job—that may work, but more often it fails. Instead, you pick the leader and go after him. He needs to be the kind of man that other men will follow.

Let your men's discipleship team leader select his own team—or at least have an equal voice with you. Together, have them implement the No Man Left Behind Model. Emphasize from the beginning that you're going after long-term, sustainable results.

The create-capture-sustain cycle rests on top of these three foundations. Think of the interactions your church has with men as a "conveyor belt"—the process of your ministry to men.

So where do you go from here?

A ONE-YEAR PLAN

Develop a one-year plan to complete one cycle (or two) of create-capture-sustain, and then reevaluate. You can start with any kind of event to create value. Then, have a short follow-up to capture the momentum. Near the end of the follow-up, offer men multiple entry points into the existing ministries of your church to sustain change.

After the inevitable drop-off predicted by the parable of the sower, the residual of new committed disciples will add to your base. Next year, you can repeat the cycle. In this way, men not "ready" this year get another opportunity. And different "types" of men can be targeted. This will give you a system to regularly invite all five types of men to connect with you when they are ready.

The beauty of the No Man Left Behind Model is that it simplifies a highly effective strategy to disciple men into a manageable process that your church can sustain. Exactly what you've always wanted!

To learn more about how to implement the No Man Left Behind Model, please see appendix A or visit *www.nomanleftbehind.org.*

POINTS TO REMEMBER

The No Man Left Behind Model: A simple yet robust model you can adopt to build an *intentional, sustainable* men's discipleship ministry to *all* of your men. You can sketch it on a paper napkin at breakfast with one of your leaders.

The "All-Inclusive" Mindset: Successful churches have a vision to disciple *all* their men, not just those willing to join "men's only" activities. So if you have 100 men in your church, that's the size of your ministry to men. And by the way, the term "men's ministry" is a spoiled term—in some places even toxic. We suggest you stop using the term "men's ministry" altogether—it can help you shed the baggage of the old wineskin that reaches only some of your men.

Five Types of Men: A "one size fits all" approach may have worked fifty years ago, but those days are long gone. In the field we find five types of men at various stages on their journeys. These five "sizes" of men fit along what we call "the wide-deep continuum." There are Men Who Need Christ, Cultural Christians, Biblical Christians, Servant Leaders, and, among each of those four groups, Hurting Men.

Clarify Your Vision: In one way or another, the essence of your vision is "to disciple every man in the church." Make sure your leaders are on the same page up front. A split or unclear vision will create a lot of discord down the road.

A Public Slogan: You will also want a "public" vision statement—a "slogan"—that resonates with your men. For example, "To help men grow as disciples and disciple-makers—starting at home." Or, "No man left behind."

An All-Inclusive Name: In addition to a clarifying the vision for the leadership team and adopting a slogan for your "public" vision statement, you will also want to come up with an "all-inclusive name"—one that unmistakably applies to *all* your men. Don't *ever* make men feel like they have to be part of your "men's only" ministry to be part of the "Men of Grace." Instead, describe *any* and *every* involvement men have with your church as something that the "Iron Men" (or whatever name you choose) are doing.

A Common Language: Since the term "disciple" can mean different things to different people, you will want to create a common language. Plan to preach a series on discipleship—something like, "What Is a Disciple, and How Do You Become One?" Focus on the biblical command to make disciples, texts that describe discipleship, and examples of discipleship that are already taking place in your church.

Create Value: You can create momentum by offering men something they want—"something of value." That may be inviting them to have breakfast, attend church, play softball, or be your guest at a special men's event.

Capture Momentum: It's so disappointing to expend all that energy to turn men out, then see them drift away when the event is over. Instead, offer what we call a "believable next right step" for the men who attend the "Success That Matters" dinner (or other event)—a step to help "capture" the momentum. For example, meeting one hour a week for six weeks to further discuss, say, "Success That Matters."

Sustain Change: This is the silver bullet—the way you can use the model to populate the new and existing growth and service ministries of your church.

At the end of the six-week groups, offer men opportunities to assimilate into the existing growth and service ministries of the church. You can also offer something new.

Repeat the Create-Capture-Sustain Cycle: The create-capture-sustain cycle is the engine that moves men along the conveyor belt. Regularly repeat the cycle with something that targets different types of men. That's how you keep it going.

The Portal Priority: Discipleship is the "portal" priority through which all the other priorities of your church can be achieved. The portal priority concept can give you and your leaders a way to filter your activities and programs to keep a tighter focus on your vision.

Your Man Code: You have an unwritten "man code" that defines what it means to be a man in your church. From the décor, to the announcements, to how men are involved in the worship service, you can create an atmosphere that says: "Men matter here. Men can make a difference. God is doing something in and through the men of this church."

Three Strands of Leadership: Successful discipleship ministries for men need strong support from the senior pastor, a committed leader, and an effective leadership team—three strands of leadership.

A One-Year Plan: Develop a one-year plan to complete one cycle (or two) of create-capture-sustain, and then reevaluate.

AFTERWORD

As you return now to your pastoring duties, may the Spirit empower you to more effectively pastor *every* willing man in your church.

I have one additional suggestion. Whatever your ministry to men will look like ten years from now will be pretty much decided at the moment you stop reading this book. So I suggest you set an appointment for yourself within the next week—for at least one hour—to start planning out the next steps of your vision, and to begin implementing any changes you want to make.

Please read appendix A for suggestions on how to take the next steps.

Finally, I really don't want our "relationship" to end. My mission, and the mission of Man in the Mirror, is to help you more effectively disciple your men. So please check out www.maninthemirror.org to consult with one of our field staff (a complimentary service) and/or to acquire extensive men's discipleship resources, most of which are free or can be acquired at cost. Also, you can sign up to receive my discipleship blog at www.PatrickMorley.com. Let's stay connected.

And now, a prayer . . .

Our dearest Father, because of his obvious desire to love and serve You, I pray You will bless this pastor with a great abundance in every area of life—his relationship with You, relationships with loved ones, work, health, finances, education, and in every other way. In the wonderful name of our Lord and Savior Jesus. For the glory of Christ and no other reason. Amen.

Until every church disciples every man…
PATRICK MORLEY

TABLE LEADERS

Each table has a leader. Each table leader has a written job description (go to the website **www.pastoringmen.com** to read it if you'd like). The table leader shows by his actions that he really *cares* about his men *personally*—that's his main responsibility. His table becomes an outlet for personal ministry. For example, some leaders want five men at their tables and some prefer a dozen. It's up to them.

After the message, he leads his men into a meaningful discussion about the topic of the day using the questions printed on the handout. We want to give men time to process, unpack, and apply the message to their lives. Our motto is, "Air time for every man every week." Table leaders should not speak more than 25 percent of the time.

Table leaders must call each man on Thursday evening every week to remind him about the meeting. Some email instead, and that's okay if it works. I know the calls sound cheesy, but when I see attendance drop off at a table over a few weeks, I sometimes walk over to the leader before we start and whisper in his ear, "Have you been making your calls?" Invariably not.

TABLE LEADER QUALIFICATIONS

We have a mixture of seasoned veterans and newer leaders. Half of our twenty-plus leaders have been with me for fifteen or more years. Whether new or veteran, this is what I look for in leaders:

- Full throttle after their own discipleship
- Passionate about seeing other men become disciples
- Wanting to shepherd a group of guys
- Members of a local church
- Attractive to the kind of men we want to reach

Also, I'm specific about what I *don't* want in leaders—those who are:

- Looking for a group to teach (We need shepherds and discussion facilitators—I've just taught a lesson, now let's discuss and apply it, not teach another lesson.)
- Short on social skills, who talk too much, and who miss important social cues
- Not willing to make—or have someone make—the weekly calls (an evidence of caring and love)

Near the beginning of the year, each table leader agrees to the terms of his job description for one year. In essence, he gets a one-year "contract." At the end of each year every table leader is out of a job! This gives both of us a time to reevaluate his commitment and effectiveness. If either one of us has a question, we discuss it candidly.

I want everyone to have a graceful exit strategy. Without an exit strategy, men hang on to their positions long after their passions and callings have changed. They lose effectiveness, but inertia keeps them from giving up their post. I would much rather have a man leave at the top of his game than have him do a half-hearted job for two or three years and lose everyone's respect.

Assuming we both want to proceed, he signs a new one-year deal. By the way, I used to allow sabbaticals, but that has never worked out. Once the flame is gone, in my experience I have never seen it return.

MEETING WITH THE TABLE LEADERS

I have always thought of the table leaders as my main ministry—my "group." Since we began, I estimate that I've discipled about a hundred men through the table leader community. Considering the model of Jesus, I have always considered this my greatest accomplishment in ministry.

The leaders gather at my home office once a month. We also have an annual half-day planning retreat. So we do have some organization behind what we do—we just don't want the men to see it! We figure that most men are already so over-calendarized and over-organized that it's nice to have a place where all they have to do is "show up." Sometimes I call it "show up" Bible study.

My friend and mentor Tom Skinner told me repeatedly, "We must become the live demonstration of the kingdom of heaven so that anytime someone wants to know what's going on in heaven, all they have to do is check with us." So the leader meetings are not "business" meetings. We meet for our own growth, to pray for each other and our men, to discuss changed lives, and for fellowship. We do an awful lot of laughing.

TREATING OUR GUESTS RIGHT

Visitors

We put business cards on each of the tables every week to invite visitors. We encourage the "regulars" to pick one up and invite someone during the week.

Each week we have three to eight visitors. "Like attracts like," so the visitors resemble the bringers.

We work hard to make the Man in the Mirror Bible Study a "safe place" for men to come and investigate the claims of Christianity. First-timers do not pay the $3.00. When they arrive, they are directed to a special table where a man welcomes them, orients them, and gives them a name tag to fill out. At the bottom of the name tag is a tear-off that includes their contact information. We send each visitor a follow-up letter or, if later in the morning they prayed to receive Christ, a special follow-up letter.

Once the meeting starts, the emcee welcomes the visitors in a low-key way. He asks them to raise their hands in unison, and the men clap to welcome them. No one gets singled out or embarrassed in any way.

After the message, I invite first-time visitors to join me at an empty table in one corner of the room. I give them the lay of the land. First, I explain the schedule—guys like to know the "agenda." Second, I explain the three kinds of men we typically see visit—*seekers, new Christians,* and *mature Christians.* Third, I ask them to share where they are on their spiritual pilgrimage.

When they share, they usually identify with one or more of the three categories I have spelled out. By the time everyone has shared, I know where they stand with Christ.

I conclude by telling the visitors we have a threefold concept. First, through the message and table discussions, we want to help men see a little larger glimpse of "the God who is." Second, we want to invite men to jettison a little piece of "the god (or gods) they have wanted." Third, because it is an application-oriented Bible study, we want to help men connect the dots—it's 9:00 a.m., the phones are ringing, and the customers are complaining. How do you make the transition? Then I invite them back and point out the second-timers' table.

If a man hasn't received Christ, I ask him if he can stay an extra ten minutes after we adjourn. They almost always do, and I share the Four Spiritual Laws booklet with them. Most receive Christ. I believe that God sends them to us because He knows we will be faithful to share the gospel with them.

Second-Timers

Many men come just once. They don't like the format, they don't like my teaching, it's too early in the morning, or they are just visiting Disney or in town on business.

That's okay. Now they know a place where they can point men they meet.

If a man does come back, he sits at the second-timers' table for one week. The main task of the second-timers' table leader is to help men get situated at a table that's "right for you." We tend to always have a new table forming, and that becomes the default location when the other tables are full.

MEN FROM ALL BACKGROUNDS

We don't really have a "Saddleback Sam" profile. From the start—I think because of Tom Skinner's influence on my life—I have always wanted the Bible study to be egalitarian. So we have always emphasized diversity. We have a bell curve distribution of men from the poorest of the poor to the richest of the rich, and from every age bracket—and they sit together at the same tables! We have also achieved a healthy dose of ethnic diversity. We haven't fully arrived, but we are a lot closer because we've tried.

ATTRITION OF MEN

Every table experiences attrition—some more, some less. Reasons run the gamut from increased church involvement, job changes, moving, or loss of interest. The shepherding skill of the table leader is certainly a main factor.

We have a Bible study administrator, who regularly asks the table leaders, "Who needs more men for their tables?" He then coordinates with the second-timers' table leader to funnel new men to those existing tables.

HOW THE BIBLE STUDY HAS CHANGED

The ministry has morphed from the early days. I would describe our *ethos* originally as "Evangelism with Discipleship and Fellowship." Today, it has morphed to "Discipleship with Fellowship and Evangelism"—no small change. We used to have new men come to Christ almost weekly. Now it's less frequent.

This happened for many reasons. First, I don't think we put as much emphasis on inviting non-Christians as we once did. Second, the messaging probably suits a growing Christian better than a seeker. Third, the percentage of men who have been attending for a long time has increased, and a lot of these men have run through their non-Christian contacts.

Fourth, the makeup of the group has morphed. Today about one-third of our men lead their own ministries—pastors, parachurch workers, elders, deacons, and lay leaders. They lead businessmen's Bible studies, home groups, run churches, teach youth and teens, operate recovery programs—you name it. Many of these men started their service because they grew in faith at the Man in the Mirror Bible Study. Others, especially pastors, have found it a great place to come and "just be a guy." We put zero emphasis on "who you are" or "what you do."

CHALLENGES TO KEEP THE PROGRAM DYNAMIC
Challenge #1
Over the years the weekly Bible study has faced several challenges. Here's the first of seven challenges we've faced and how we adapted in response.

In the early 1990s I just about destroyed the whole deal. I got on this kick that we needed to discover all our problems and fix them. For month after tedious month, I led the table leaders into a death spiral. It was downright depressing to them. After a while, I got depressed too.

Then one day I remembered that men were regularly coming to Christ and that the table leaders were deeply impacting many of the men at their tables. We changed the focus from "fixing our problems" to "discussing changed lives." We started spending our time talking about what God was doing in men's lives. I swore to never again surface a problem unless it really was a problem. Within days things started to look exciting again—and still do!

Challenge #2
With the busy "ten talent" men we have as leaders, I always considered two-thirds attendance at leader meetings to be great—roughly equal to the Rotary's perfect attendance. At about the fifteen-year mark, though, table leader attendance at the then twice-monthly meetings dropped from about two-thirds (or more) to about one-half (or less). I didn't know what to make of it—or whether to take it personally. On one hand, the Bible study was cooking right along, so why upset the apple cart? On the other hand, it says right in the job descriptions they sign that they will attend!

Eventually I realized that the "burnout clock" for table leader meetings must start ticking before the "burnout clock" for leading a table on Friday mornings. Some of those leaders had been with me for a dozen or more years! One day when I was praying about it, the Lord spoke to my heart and said, "Love them more." A strange answer, for sure, but that's what I did. Looking back on it, I'm quite sure

I would have completely destroyed the Bible study if I had tried to force their attendance. Of course, if a table leader doesn't attend leader meetings and his table falls off, that's a whole different story.

At the twenty-year mark (after five years of "love them more"), nothing had changed. The leader meeting attendance was still down to 50 percent (and sometimes less). I figured, *Maybe it's just too much to ask.* So we dropped from twice monthly to once monthly. Do you think it helped? Frankly, I like it better, but it didn't make a twit of difference in attendance.

Then someone had the idea of requiring table leaders to attend *or send a man* from their tables. The meetings would be full, the visitors would catch a whole different vision for the Bible study, and potential leaders could be groomed. It worked for a while, but it was an idea that just didn't want to work long term.

It is easy to look at the data and come to the wrong conclusion. It's easy to go off half-cocked and solve the wrong problem.

I knew that the devil would like nothing better than for me to "blow up" our very successful Friday morning Bible study over the table leader meeting attendance issue.

I knew I needed to wait on the Lord to clarify the problem, but now several years had gone by. Finally the issue did clarify. I could find no correlation between leader attendance at the meetings and success at leading a table on Friday mornings. Quite the contrary, the men who didn't attend leader meetings all had awesome tables on Friday morning. So they didn't *really* need to be at the leader meetings from that standpoint. At the same time, leaders who are not "plugged in" are ripe to get picked off.

Here's the solution: Together, the table leaders and I decided the Man in the Mirror Bible Study and the table leader meetings are "two separate ministries" (versus "one ministry with two parts"). We decided a table leader doesn't have to attend the monthly leader meetings *provided* he is part of some other group that provides a measure of accountability. But I love the monthly meetings—it's my "table"—so anyone who wants me to be their "table leader" can come to the monthly meetings.

And, best of all, God gave us the wisdom to not blow up a perfectly good ministry over an issue easily, if not quickly, solved in a different way.

Challenge #3

From time to time, the "burnout clock" runs out before the job description expires. When that happens—which is not very often—I have a special email that I send. I call it my "Dear George" letter:

> Dear George,
>
> I've noticed (I think) that your table has dwindled. We need to decide what to do to rebuild it. Before that, however, I need to know how you are feeling about it.
>
> Over the years we've seen tables decline for two major reasons:
> 1. The normal attrition of men as they move on to other things.
> 2. The priorities of the table leader change.
>
> Before we rebuild the table, I would like to know if you still feel this is a calling and priority. The best way for you to assess that is to ask yourself three questions:
>
> 1. Have I been faithful to call my men? (This is probably the best "litmus test" for men to know "for sure" that you care about them personally.)
> 2. Have I led my men into meaningful discussions about the topics of the day with balanced participation? (This skill of drawing men out and the leader not talking too much is a "make or break" issue.)
> 3. Have I been faithful to the table leader job description? (Best answered by looking it over in a spirit of prayer.)
>
> My love for you, George, is unconditional and does not depend in any way on which way you want to go. You don't have to be a table leader to make me happy. I do have a responsibility, though, to make sure this is something you are truly committed to before we start rebuilding.
>
> Why don't you think this over prayerfully and let me know.
>
> Serving Christ together,
> Pat

Sometimes a table leader's calling changes, and he doesn't even recognize it. I took one leader to breakfast to talk about his table. He had found a new passion that he was hard after. He was feeling guilty for not doing a better job as a table leader—and his table had dwindled. But he didn't want to leave the table! I proposed that we celebrate his past success and new calling, and let him return with dignity to non-leader status. He agreed, and a relationship was saved by dealing with it head-on.

Challenge #4

Why have our numbers not grown since 1990? I really like our size. It's big, but not too big. In order to grow we would have to move to a bigger facility. But with our value of "working ourselves out of a job with every man," we would rather have men "flow through" into churches than accumulate.

After a man can stand on his own two feet spiritually, we want to pass him off so he can get his family vitally connected into the life of a local church. We have seen over 3,000 men come through! Most have become better leaders in their families. Many have also become leaders for Christ's church—pastors, missionaries, parachurch workers, elders, deacons, teachers, and evangelists.

But God has outwitted us on size because, in 2001, one of our table leaders started webcasting the Bible study, and now we have thousands of downloads every week in every state and in thirty-eight countries. Each week small groups around the world watch the videos and print out the same discussion questions we use on Fridays.

Also, *The Man in the Mirror* book and Man in the Mirror Ministries grew out of the Bible study. Since its founding in 1991, Man in the Mirror has impacted over ten million men worldwide. Everything we do flows from The Man in the Mirror Bible Study. It's the incubator where new ideas get hatched—the laboratory where we experiment (and, usually, I am the laboratory rat upon whom God performs His experiments!).

Challenge #5

Around 2005 we started to find it difficult to recruit new table leaders who took 2 Timothy 2:2 seriously. Our solution was to start a "leadership development" table that runs for six weeks twice a year. Frankly, most of the graduates wanted the training for their "other" ministries, so we decided to encourage that too. We also have graduated some fine men as new table leaders, and now our leaders get up to speed much faster than before we did the training.

Challenge #6

Making the weekly reminder calls has always been a "sticking point" for some of our table leaders. It's ironic that the single greatest predictor of attendance—a reminder phone call—is the single greatest weakness for many leaders (sometimes it's hard not to admire the devil's cleverness).

I don't blame them. Calling leaders to remind them of our monthly leaders meeting is pure drudgery for me—it's too routine, structured, and another thing I "have" to do. So I have a man who loves to make the calls. The table leaders can also get a man at their tables to make the calls.

The reminder is a means, not an end, so I don't want the tail to wag the dog. Some table leaders can turn their men out with an email reminder—so be it. A couple of leaders have men so faithful and disciplined that they don't need nor, in some cases, do they want a reminder call. That's fine. At the end of the day, what we really want is for each man to feel like somebody really cares about them personally.

Challenge #7

I know this will sound amazing, but for almost two decades we had thirty to fifty men each week not pay the $3.00 to cover the room rental at the civic center. On more than one occasion I have stood next to the "honor system" money basket and watch a man walk in, greet me warmly, look me straight in the eye, and then walk right by the basket! On the bright side, we must be attracting the kind of men who need to hear God's Word!

For most of those years, the coffee and donuts were donated by one of our men who owned a Dunkin' Donut franchise (effectively subsidizing the cheaters!). He sold his business, so in 2007 we had to start paying for coffee and donuts.

The problem was easily resolved. We manned the table with a cashier. I announced that if the money was a problem for anyone we would waive the $3.00, and two or three men took up that offer.

DISTINCTIVES AND VALUES

Together, the table leaders and I have forged a common set of beliefs about God's calling for our Bible study. What's important to us—the distinctives and values that make it work—include the following:

- Grace: an oasis where men can come at the end of the week and get a drink; men deserve grace just for showing up; show men Christ versus fix their behavior; unconditional acceptance
- Making disciples: grace-based, application-oriented teaching; change core affections of the heart; heart transformation, not behavior modification
- Changed lives: we measure our profits in changed lives
- Table groups: a place where men care about each other personally; the relationship is the task; a hub that extends beyond the Bible study; all tables are "open," but deep relationships develop
- Discussion time: at tables after the teaching to flesh out and apply the message; air time for every man every week
- Hurting men: a hospital for men with broken wings; a warming hut at the base of the ski slope; we want men to "feel the love"
- Egalitarian: a cross section of our community; multi-denominational; multi-ethnic
- Low barriers; no preparation required, just show up
- Visitors encouraged: welcomed but not put on the spot; "multiple" personal invitations required; a process to assimilate
- We are a Bible study, not a church: we want to work ourselves out of a job, see men get involved in a church
- Leaders passionate about discipling men: full throttle after their own discipleship; make weekly reminder calls for Friday a.m.; shepherds not teachers
- Table leader community: table leaders meet monthly for study, prayer, and fellowship; annual half-day planning retreat

CAN THIS MODEL BE REPRODUCED IN A CHURCH?

While ours is a "community" Bible study, the largest Bible studies in America take place in churches—typically mornings for churches in the suburbs and lunch for the downtown churches. But the location is secondary. What's primary is a passion to see men become disciples.

Take East Cooper Baptist Church, a church of 2,300 adults, in Mt. Pleasant, South Carolina, for example. After visiting the Man in the Mirror Bible Study as part of a No Man Left Behind Conference here in Orlando, their team went home and replicated the Bible study in their church. Here's how layman Randy Bates describes it:

We came back and planned for a fall introduction of the Friday morning study, which we call Man2Man. We purchased 25 round tables to facilitate the discussions after the message.

Within a short time 70 men were regularly attending each week. During our second year we averaged about 105 men and, in year three, we averaged around 145 men.

We started with donuts like you do, but soon ramped up a full hot breakfast of eggs, bacon, sausage, biscuits, gravy, grits, hash browns, oatmeal, fruit, cereal, coffee, and juice. Food comes on at 6:20 a.m., I start the announcements at 6:40 a.m., and pray by 6:50 a.m. Our pastor, Conrad "Buster" Brown, speaks until 7:10 a.m., and then we have table talk until 7:35 a.m. Most men can be at work by 8:00 a.m.

The good news is not about the numbers—it's the fact that we are changing men's lives, and we're getting a lot of positive comments from the women at the church.

Frankly, growing the study beyond a dozen men is also secondary.

Here are the primary factors that need to be addressed if you want to start a similar Bible study:

- Vision: A vision to make disciples
- Environment: A welcoming, grace-oriented attitude and environment
- Love: Men respond when they feel like we care; especially keep an eye out for men who are hurting
- Messaging: A relevant, application-oriented message prepared especially for men presented by a decent speaker and followed by time to discuss it
- Barriers: Low barriers to attend (e.g., no homework—you can graduate men into deeper studies later)
- Visitors: A "visitors welcome" culture
- Systematic: Men love things that run smoothly

If you do grow, then you will need a table leaders level, but that can come later. When that happens, here are two more factors to address:

- Table groups: For men to connect "with a few" and do life together

- Table leaders: Form a community of leaders passionate about discipling men who can build strong relationships at the tables

Of course, if you start a study, you will develop your own vision, mission, distinctives, and values; but this gives you a proven baseline from which to begin. To receive a copy of Chris White's "How to Build a Dynamic Men's Fellowship," email me at patrickmorley@maninthemirror.org.

APPENDIX C

WIDE ---------- Discipleship CONTINUUM ---------- DEEP

#1—NEED CHRIST	#2—CULTURAL CHRISTIAN	#3—BIBLICAL DISCIPLE	#4—LEADER or APPRENTICE Leader
Life Focus = *ME*	Life Focus = *Me & God*	Life Focus = *GOD & Me*	Life Focus = *God & Others*
CALLED 2 "live **IN** Christ"	*EQUIPPED* 2 "live **LIKE** Christ"	Equipped "**MORE** like Christ"	*SENT* 2 "live **FOR** Christ"
"HANGING OUT" Open Group/Drop-In Format **Low** Commitment **No** Prep	*"COMMON GROUND"* Open Group/Drop-In Format **Some** Commitment **Some** Prep	*"NEXT STEPS"* Semi-Open Group **More** Commitment **More** Prep	*"ALLIES & APPRENTICES"* Closed Group **High** Commitment **Much** Prep
Outreach Venues	**Fellowship Venues**	**Discipleship Venues**	**Leadership Venues**
"Man Cave" TV Viewing Parties Auto Fair/Car Show/ Racing Venues Father's Day Outing— Baseball Game Sporting Venues— complimentary tickets Outdoorsmen— Hiking/Camping/etc.	Hobbies & Interest Survey Men's Conference Father-Daughter Summit Financial Peace University Service Projects	Spiritual Life Survey In-Depth Studies Spiritual Disciplines Regional Mission Trips Threefold Cords (Ecc. 4:12)	Small Group Coleaders Specialized Training Seminars Leadership Summit— FUEL/NCMM International Mission Trips Ministry Experience/ Apprenticeships
"Recruiting Station"	*"Army of Men"*	*"Band of Brothers"*	*"Foxhole Friends"*
Exploration Group	**Discussion Group**	**Application Group**	**Mobilization Group**
"Is Christianity 4 You?" Pat Morley	*"Man In The Mirror"* Pat Morley	*"How God Makes Men"* Pat Morley	*"No Man Left Behind"* M/D/C
"The Reason 4 God" Tim Keller	*"Man Alive"* Pat Morley	*"Measure of a Man"* Gene Getz	*"Men Hate Going to Church"* David Murrrow
"The Case 4 Christ" Lee Strobel	*"7 Seasons"* Pat Morley	*"Man's Guide 2 Spiritual Disciplines"*	*"Sleeping Giant"* Kenny Luck
"More Than A Carpenter" Josh McDowell	*"Game Plan 4 Life"* Joe Gibbs	*"Kingdom Man"* Tony Evans	*"Experiencing God"* Henry Blackaby
"Can Man Live w/o God" Ravi Zacharias	*"Man's Guide 2 Work"* Pat Morley	*"Wild At Heart"* John Eldredge	*"Prayer"* Philip Yancey
"Mere Christianity" C. S. Lewis	*"Life You've Always Wanted"* Ortberg	*"Radical"* David Platt	*"Missional Renaissance"* McNeal
"John 3:16" Max Lucado	*"Halftime"* Bob Buford	*"Tender Warrior"* Stu Weber	*"Post-Church Christian"* Paul Nyquist

#5 - HURTING MEN			
Life Focus = Where is *God?*			
Ministry of "Hanging Out" Motor Racing Outreach *"Power of Encouragement"* David Jeremiah *Celebrate Recovery* Saddleback	*"When God Doesn't Make Sense"* James Dobson *"When Bad Christians Happen to Good People"* Dave Burchett	*"Traveling Light"* Max Lucado *"Grace Awakening"* Chuck Swindoll *"Fathered by God"* John Eldredge	*"Boundaries"* Cloud/Townsend *"Great House of God"* Max Lucado *"A Place Called Blessing"* John Trent

WIDE ---------- **Discipleship CONTINUUM** ---------- **DEEP**

#1—NEED CHRIST	#2—CULTURAL CHRISTIAN	#3—BIBLICAL DISCIPLE	#4—LEADER or APPRENTICE Leader
Life Focus = *ME*	Life Focus = *Me & God*	Life Focus = *GOD & Me*	Life Focus = *God & Others*

What is *already happening* in your church setting?

Outreach Venues	Fellowship Venues	Discipleship Venues	Leadership Venues

What *could be happening* in your church setting?

Outreach Venues	Fellowship Venues	Discipleship Venues	Leadership Venues

#5—HURTING MEN	#5—HURTING MEN	#5—HURTING MEN	#5—HURTING MEN

Life Focus = *Where is God?*

Names:	Names:	Names:	Names:

NOTES

CHAPTER 1: IS PASTORING MEN WORTH THE EFFORT?

1. Eighty percent of men are so emotionally impaired, Terrence Real, *I Don't Want to Talk About It* (New York: Fireside, 1997), 56.
2. Sixty percent of men are in financial trouble, Howard Dayton, personal correspondence with the author, 2004.
3. Fifty percent of men who attend church, "Pornography Statistics," Family Safe Media, www.familysafemedia.com/pornography_statistics.html. I once spoke at a Christian meeting of 500 men who were asked if they had actively sought out pornography within the previous year. Approximately 60 percent of the men wrote *yes* on a slip of paper and dropped it into a basket on their way to a break.
4. Forty percent of men get divorced, American Academy of Pediatrics, "Family Pediatrics Report of the Task Force on the Family," *Pediatrics* 111, no. 6 (2003): 1541–71.
5. Retrieved at www.usatoday.com/news/health/2007-09-19-divorce-census_N.htm.
6. Casey E. Copen, Kimberly Daniels, and William D. Mosher, "First Premarital Cohabitation in the United States: 2006–2010 National Survey of Family Growth," *National Health Statistics Reports,* no. 64, April 4, 2013, www.cdc.gov/nchs/data/nhsr/nhsr064.pdf.
7. "Unmarried Childbearing," Centers for Disease Control and Prevention, January 2013, www.cdc.gov/nchs/fastats/unmarry.htm. Children living in homes without their biological fathers: Rose M. Kreider, *Living Arrangements of Children: 2004,* Household Economics Studies, US Census Bureau, February 2008, www.census.gov/prod/2008pubs/p70-114.pdf.
8. Retrieved at http://link.springer.com/article/10.1007%2Fs11205-007-9149-8?LI=true#page-1.
9. Karen Pazol et al., "Abortion Surveillance—United States, 2009," *Morbidity and Mortality Weekly Report,* Centers for Disease Control and Prevention, November 23, 2012, www.cdc.gov/mmwr/preview/mmwrhtml/ss6108a1.htm?s_cid=ss6108a1_w.
10. American Academy of Pediatrics, "Family Pediatrics Report of The Task Force on the Family," *Pediatrics,* 111(2003): 1541–71.

CHAPTER 2: HOW ARE YOUR MEN DOING?

1. Roy F. Baumeister, Oxford: Oxford University Press, 2010, e-book location 560.
2. The Greek word Paul uses translated "frustration" is the same word the Septuagint selected to translate Solomon's "meaningless" from Hebrew to Greek. Hence, Paul and Solomon meant the same thing. *Meaningless, frustration*, and *futility* are synonyms.

CHAPTER 3: WHAT DO MEN WANT?

1. Michael Novak, *Business as a Calling* (New York: The Free Press, 1996), 29.
2. Viktor E. Frankl, *Man's Search for Meaning* (New York: Simon and Schuster: 1984), 107.
3. Ibid., 105.
4. W. R. Moody, *The Life of Dwight L. Moody* (Westwood, OH: Barbour), 122.
5. C. S. Lewis, *God in the Dock* (Grand Rapids, MI: Eerdmans, 1970), 280.

CHAPTER 4: WHAT KEEPS MEN FROM GETTING WHAT THEY WANT?

1. C. S. Lewis, *The Weight of Glory* (New York: Simon and Schuster, 1962), 15–16.
2. Michael Novak, *Business As a Calling* (New York: The Free Press, 1996), 29.
3. Francis A. Schaeffer, *How Should We Then Live?* (Westchester, IL: Crossway, 1976), 205.
4. For the story of Walt O. and the Meloon family business, see James Vincent, *Parting the Waters* (Chicago: Moody, 1997).
5. Patrick Morley, *The Man in the Mirror* (Grand Rapids, MI: Zondervan, 1989), 33.

CHAPTER 5: WHAT DO MEN NEED AND HOW CAN YOU GIVE IT TO THEM?

1. Population Statistics: Table 7, "Resident Population Projections by Age and Sex, 1980 to 2006, U.S. Census Bureau," retrieved from www.census.org/compendia/statab/tables/08s0007.pdf. We use fifteen for manhood because this is the age when young men tend to get a job and the car keys. Earning money and driving a 3,000-pound vehicle is as good a way as any to determine adulthood.
2. An estimate based on 39 percent indicating they are "born again"; retrieved from Barna Group at www.barna.org/cgi-bin/Pagecategory.asp?CategoryID+19.
3. Pastor Rogers told me this story during a telephone conversation a few years ago.
4. *Brother Lawrence of the Resurrection*, trans. John J. Delaney, "The Practice of the Presence of God" (New York: Doubleday,1977), 108.

CHAPTER 7: SUCCESS FACTORS IN DISCIPLING MEN

1. Arthur D. Little and McKinsey & Co. studies cited in Peter M. Senge, Art Kleiner, Charlotte Roberts, and George Roth, *The Dance of Change* (New York: Doubleday, 1999), 5; Business Intelligence study cited in D. Miller, "Successful Change Leaders," *Journal of Change Management* 2, no. 4 (2002): 360; Gartner Group study cited in Miller, 2002; A. Raps, "Implementing Startegy," *Strategic Finance* 85(12):49–53 (2004). This appears to be the case without regard to sector; whether public, private, for profit, nonprofit, business, government, education, or health care (e.g., P. Strebel, "Why Do Employees Resist Change?", *Harvard Business Review* 74, no. 3 [2000] 86–92; P. Pluye, L. Potvin, and J. Denis, "Making Public Health Programs Last: Conceptualizing Sustainability," *Evaluation & Program Planning* 27, no. 2 [2004]: 121–33).
2. Booz Allen Hamilton, *New Products Management for the 1980s*. (This consulting firm published their findings in 1982; obtained from secondary sources.)
3. S. Ogawa and F. Piller, *MIT Sloan Management Review*, "Reducing the risks of new product development," 47, no. 2 (Winter 2006): 65.
4. Jim Collins, *Good to Great* (New York: Harper Business, 2001).
5. Philip Thurston, "Should Smaller Companies Make Formal Plans?" *Harvard Business Review*, September–October 1983.
6. Collins, *Good to Great*, 21–22.

CHAPTER 8: MORE SUCCESS FACTORS IN DISCIPLING MEN

1. Billy Graham, "My Answer: Jesus' Methods Would Be Up-To-Date Today," *Christian Post*, February 11, 2008, retrieved from Internet February 11, 2008.
2. Robert Lewis with Rob Wilkins, *The Church of Irresistible Influence* (Grand Rapids: Zondervan, 2001).

CHAPTER 9: THE NO MAN LEFT BEHIND MODEL

1. F. Okumus, "A Framework to Implement Strategies in Organizations," *Management Decision*, 41 no. 9 (2003): 871–82.
2. Estimate based on results after eight years of intense effort by Rev. Jeff Kisiah, a dedicated "men's" pastor at Harvest Community Church, Charlotte, North Carolina. Other anecdotal reports corroborate.
3. Note: While this chapter focuses on learning this model for men's discipleship, please consider applying the "perspective" of managing momentum to every area of your ministry.

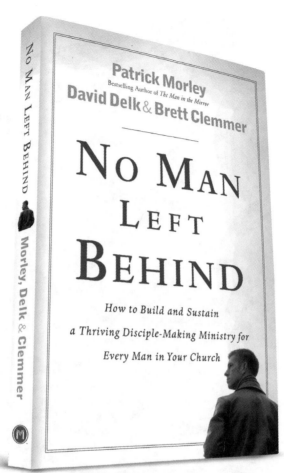

ISBN: 978-0-8024-7549-7

David Murrow's book *Why Men Hate Going to Church* has heightened awareness of an epidemic—Patrick Morley offers the solution. *No Man Left Behind* is the blueprint for growing a thriving men's ministry that has the power to rebuild the church as we know it, pulling men off the couch and into active involvement as part of the body of Christ.

Also available as an eBook

MOODY
Publishers™

From the Word to Life

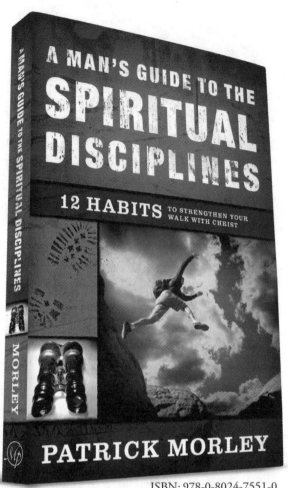

ISBN: 978-0-8024-7551-0

———————————

S trength isn't something you wish for; it's something you work toward. We need more than an annual men's gathering and regular church attendance to keep our faith strong. Here are the tools men need to reflect Christ in the context of marriage, family, and the daily grind.

Also available as an eBook

MOODY
Publishers™

*From the Word **to** Life*

Books from A. W. Tozer:

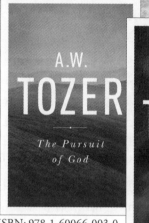

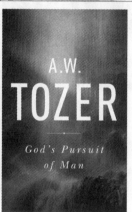

ISBN: 978-1-60066-003-0

ISBN: 978-1-60066-795-4

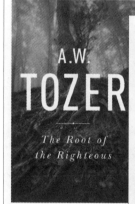

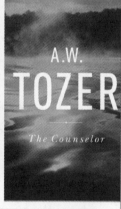

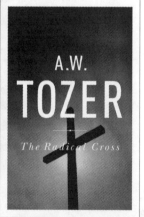

ISBN: 978-1-60066-797-8

ISBN: 978-1-60066-796-1

ISBN: 978-1-60066-050-4

Also available as eBooks

MOODY
Publishers

From the Word to Life

*From the Word **to Life***

Moody Radio produces and delivers compelling programs filled with biblical insights and creative expressions of faith that help you take the next step in your relationship with Christ.

You can hear Moody Radio on 36 stations and more than 1,500 radio outlets across the U.S. and Canada. Or listen on your smartphone with the Moody Radio app!

www.moodyradio.org